Prospect Research Fundamentals

Proven Methods to Help Charities Realize
More Major Gifts

FOURTH EDITION

Elizabeth Dollhopf-Brown, Editor

WILEY

978-1-118-69041-3   ISBN

978-1-118-70382-3   ISBN (online)

Prospect Research Fundamentals

Proven Methods to Help Charities Realize More Major Gifts

Edited by
Elizabeth Dollhopf-Brown

Elizabeth Dollhopf-Brown offers expertise in leading research, relationship management and analytics teams strategically partnered with campaign and development colleagues to maximize fundraising effectiveness.

She has over 10 years of development experience and has served as the Senior Director of Research and Prospect Management at the University of Rochester since 2008. Previously, she was the Director of Prospect Analysis and Research at Marquette University in Milwaukee, Wisconsin. Before she was drawn to research and relationship management, her passion was for annual giving, where she headed the Marquette Fund and worked in Annual Giving at DePauw University in Greeencastle, Indiana.

She is a graduate of Susquehanna University and received her MBA from Marquette. A frequent speaker, she is APRA's (Association of Professional Researchers for Advancement) 2012-2013 President and has previously served as the Chair of APRA's Education and Professional Development committee and Conference Chair.

Published by

Stevenson, Inc.
P.O. Box 4528 • Sioux City, Iowa • 51104
Phone 712.239.3010 • Fax 712.239.2166
www.stevensoninc.com

Prospect Research Fundamentals: Proven Methods to Help Charities Realize More Major Gifts, Fourth Edition.
Edited by Elizabeth Dollhopf-Brown.
© 2012 Stevenson, Inc. Published 2012 by Stevenson, Inc.

THE ETHICS OF PROSPECT RESEARCH

All research, in fact all fundraising practices and related practices, should be conducted in a manner which is based on a foundation of ethical principles. True philanthropy is the outcome of acts of kindness and goodness. Nothing less should be expected of us who are in the business of seeking and inviting such acts of kindness. Remember and live by The Golden Rule in all that you do: "One should treat others as one would like others to treat oneself."

APRA Statement of Ethics *(Copyright 2009 APRA)*

Association of Professional Researchers for Advancement (APRA) members shall support and further the individual's fundamental right to privacy and protect the confidential information of their institutions. APRA members are committed to the ethical collection and use of information. Members shall follow all applicable national, state, and local laws, as well as institutional policies, governing the collection, use, maintenance, and dissemination of information in the pursuit of the missions of their institutions.

Code of Ethics

Advancement researchers must balance an individual's right to privacy with the needs of their institutions to collect, analyze, record, maintain, use, and disseminate information. This balance is not always easy to maintain. To guide researchers, the following ethical principles apply:

I. Fundamental Principles

Four fundamental principles provide the foundation for the ethical conduct of fundraising research, relationship management, and analytics: integrity, accountability, practice, and conflict of interest.

A. Integrity

Members shall be truthful with respect to their identities and purpose and the identity of their institutions during the course of their work. They shall continually strive to increase the recognition and respect of the profession.

B. Accountability

Members shall respect the privacy of donors and prospects and conduct their work with the highest level of discretion. They shall adhere to the spirit as well as the letter of all applicable laws and all policies of their organization. They shall conduct themselves in the utmost professional manner in accordance with the standards of their organization.

C. Practice

Members shall take the necessary care to ensure that their work is as accurate as possible. They shall only record data that is appropriate to the fundraising process and protect the confidentiality of all personal information at all times.

D. Conflicts of Interest

Members shall avoid competing professional or personal interests and shall disclose such interests to their institutions at the first instance. A conflict of interest can create an appearance of impropriety that can undermine confidence in the member, their organization, and the profession.

II. Standards of Practice

A. Collection

1. The collection of information should be done lawfully, respecting applicable laws and institutional policies.

2. Advancement researchers should be experts on the reliability of sources (print, electronic and otherwise), as well as the sources utilized by third parties to gather information on their behalf.

3. Advancement researchers should not evade or avoid questions about their affiliations or purpose when requesting information in person, over the phone, electronically or in writing. It is recommended that requests for public information be made on institutional stationery and that these requests clearly identify the requestor.

4. Advancement researchers should use the usual and customary methods of payment or reimbursement for products or services purchased on behalf of their institutions.

5. Advancement researchers who are employed full-time for an institution and also perform consulting services should develop clear understandings with their primary employers about the use of the employer's financial and human resources.

continued on page 5

continued from page 4

B. Recording and Maintenance

1. Advancement researchers shall present information in an objective and factual manner; note attribution and clearly identify information which is conjecture or analysis. Where there is conflicting information, advancement researchers should objectively present the multiple versions and state any reason for preferring one version over another.

2. Advancement researchers should develop security measures to protect the constituent information to which they have access from access by unauthorized persons. When possible, these measures should include locking offices and/or file cabinets, and secure and frequently changed passwords to electronic databases. Advancement researchers should also advocate institution-wide policies which promote the careful handling of constituent information so that constituent privacy is protected. The use of constituent databases over a wireless Internet connection is not recommended.

3. Where advancement researchers are also responsible for donor giving records and their maintenance, they should develop security measures to provide very limited access to the giving records of anonymous donors. Access to these records should be limited to only those staff who need the information to successfully cultivate, solicit or steward said donor.

4. Where there is no existing case law which outlines clearly the rights of a donor in accessing advancement files (paper and/or electronic), advancement researchers should work with their institution's legal counsel to develop an institution specific policy regarding this access. This policy should be put in writing, approved by the president/CEO, and distributed to any advancement professionals who might field a request for such access.

5. When electronic or paper documents pertaining to constituents must be disposed of, they should be disposed of in a fashion which lessens the danger of a privacy breach. Shredding of paper documents is recommended.

C. Use and Distribution

1. Researchers shall adhere to all applicable laws, as well as to institutional policies, regarding the use and distribution of confidential constituent information. Careful consideration should be given to the use of electronic mail and faxes for the delivery of constituent information.

2. Constituent information is the property of the institution for which it was collected and shall not be given to persons other than those who are involved with the cultivation or solicitation effort or those who need that information in the performance of their duties for that institution.

3. Constituent information for one institution shall not be taken to another institution.

4. Research documents containing constituent information that is to be used outside research offices shall be clearly marked *confidential.*

5. Vendors, consultants and other external entities shall understand and agree to comply with the institution's confidentiality policies before gaining access to institutional data.

6. Advancement researchers, with the assistance of institutional counsel and the advancement chief officer, should develop policies which address the sharing of directory information on their constituents with other institutions. Constituent requests to withhold directory information should be respected in all cases.

Confidentiality and Privacy Issues

Personal privacy and the confidentiality of donor records are topics that elicit a great deal of discussion. Some state-funded institutions, especially colleges and universities, are battling their local governments for ownership of the information. Vital tools in this atmosphere are well-documented policies and procedures which address the various types and sources of requests for information. If you do not have a written policy and procedures statement, you can use the following points to guide you in the development of one.

Paper Files

- Determine who is allowed to view your files; limit both internal and external requests.

- Detail not only who has access, but the procedures for everyone to follow. Include a checkout policy, which states the time limits and location restrictions.

- Are files allowed outside your office or building?

- What procedures should be followed for returning files?

- Who is responsible for managing the files' access?

Databases

- Ascertain the appropriate personnel for online access to your database. Make sure everyone with access is aware of all policies and security issues. You may even want them to sign a contract.

- You should have a separate section in the policy covering requests for biographical information. Addresses, phone numbers, birth dates, e-mail addresses and even educational degree records may be considered confidential, and you need to document who has access to that data and how it is disbursed.

- Are stalker laws applicable to your situation? Be aware of both sides of the issue; some individuals do not want others to know where they live, while others would be glad to hear from an old friend. Can you fulfill the request and still maintain confidentiality by forwarding a letter to the person the requestor is trying to locate?

- Gift and pledge information access policies should be well-thought-out. Determine your need to balance publicity with the wishes of your donors. Do you

ever release anonymous gift information, and if so, to whom?

- If you publish an honor roll, are gift amounts or ranges included? How is the honor roll distributed and to whom?

- Familiarize yourself with the legal issues for your state and organization. How do the Freedom of Information Act (FIA) and Health Insurance Portability and Accountability Act (HIPAA) affect you, and what are the penalties for noncompliance? Do you release lists of specific donors and their gifts to journalists?

- Who is responsible for managing access and determining the legitimacy of the requests? What procedures do you have in place for dealing with access issues?

Information Distribution

- Aside from the access methods discussed above, you should document your policies and procedures for disbursing information through lists, labels and computer media.

- Do you have a special computer request form designed? Is the data produced at a cost which is passed on to the requestor?

- When you distribute the information in these formats, make sure you include a confidentiality and appropriate use statement. It could be a form the person receiving the data has to sign, or a label that indicates receipt of the information implies acceptance of the policy and terms.

- If you provide the data on a computer disk, do you limit the formats?

- Will you provide technical support for those who have difficulty processing the data on their computers?

While privacy issues have always been of concern to those who deal with confidential records, technological advances and the publicity they have received have created greater concern among a wider audience. Make sure your organization is on solid ground by documenting your policies and procedures.

The Ethics of Social Media Prospect Research

Say you learn of a major prospect's favorite restaurant through a Facebook update, political affiliation through a LinkedIn profile or business transaction through a Twitter tweet. Should such information be added to that individual's donor profile?

"It's a challenging issue. There's a lot of gray area when it comes to social media," says Messellech Abebe, a client service consultant at Wealth Engine (Bethesda, MD). "This new layer of information is bringing to a head a whole new set of ethical issues."

Abebe says these ambiguities can best be addressed with clear policies and procedures that guide the use of social media in prospect research. "Nonprofits often jump on the social media bandwagon to keep up with current trends, and fail to understand the ramifications of trying to operate without any written guidelines."

Because nonprofits often don't know where to start, Abebe offers these best practices for social media ethics:

Step 1: Set a Policy

✓ Define what is considered confidential. Information gathered piece-by-piece from the Internet might not seem confidential, but when compiled into a robust donor profile, it absolutely is, says Abebe.

✓ Delineate who has access to confidential information and enforce those restrictions.

✓ Set parameters for information gathering. What kind of information will be taken from what social media sources? Make decisions on things like marital status, religion, political affiliation and sexual orientation, on principle and well before information on any particular donor has come to light.

✓ Write your decisions into a policy and then read it, know it and live it. Without a policy in writing, ethical and procedural complications will become a continual drag on development staff, says Abebe.

✓ Represent yourself honestly. Don't misrepresent yourself or your purpose when seeking prospect information through social media networks.

Step 2: Use a Confidentiality Statement

✓ Have everyone who handles confidential information (staff, faculty, volunteers, students) sign the statement, and make sure that, at the very least, it outlines what kinds of information can and can't be shared publicly.

✓ Include sections of the APRA Statement of Ethics and Donor Bill of Rights in the confidentiality statement. These documents provide examples of useful and appropriate language that can be referenced when drafting a first-time statement, says Abebe.

Step 3: Follow Security Procedures

✓ Institute procedures for both online and hardcopy documents.

✓ Clearly mark files Confidential. Noting pieces of information that came from social media platforms is a good idea as well, says Abebe.

✓ Lock up hardcopy documents in secure filing cabinets.

✓ Be wary of transmitting information via e-mail and fax. One of the easiest security strategies is password protecting sensitive files. Using secure, online or encrypted fax services can provide additional security.

✓ Shred documents no longer needed. Abebe suggests a quarterly office clean-out day to process confidential documents and dispose of those that are no longer needed.

Source: Messellech "Selley" Abebe, Client Service Consultant, Wealth Engine, Bethesda, MD. E-mail: mabebe@wealthengine.com

Prospect Research Fundamentals — 4th Edition

Knowing where to begin in the research process can be a daunting task. That's why it's important to understand your department's strengths and weaknesses and to have clear objectives in mind as you strive to build and improve your research efforts. This chapter should help you with the basics and point you to useful references.

10 Questions Prospect Management Systems Should Answer

Is your prospect management system ensuring that the right solicitor asks the right prospect for the right amount supporting the right program at the right time? Or are you just recording contact reports, asks Christina Pulawski, principle of Christina Pulawski Consulting (Chicago, IL).

Pulawski says a prospect management system is not a way to measure things — contacts, visits, etc. — but rather "a system of managing the identification, cultivation, solicitation and stewardship of prospective donors through strategic actions designed to move each prospect toward the fullest possible relationship with your organization."

Pulawski says a management system should be able to answer specific, practical questions such as:

1. How many prospects are in the solicitation pipeline?

2. How many major gifts are being solicited or planned?

3. How many of those solicitations were successful? What is our yield?

4. How many prospects have been identified for specific projects?

5. What proportion of dollars is actually being raised through development efforts?

6. How much revenue can be projected for a year or campaign?

7. How are staff performing against goals?

8. What activities are most effective with different types of prospects?

9. Are there enough prospects to meet organizational needs?

10. Are quality major gift prospects being neglected?

Source: Christina Pulawski, Principle, Christina Pulawski Consulting, Chicago, IL. E-mail: c-pulawski@comcast.net

Consider All Prospects as Wealthy Until Proven Otherwise

How does your organization define major gift? $10,000? $50,000? $100,000?

Whatever amount you choose as your major gift threshold, recognize that every one of your constituents should be considered a major gift prospect until proven otherwise.

As you narrow prospect lists to that handful of persons capable of making major gifts, be aware that incorrect judgments may cause you to rule out individuals and businesses with the ability to make major gifts. After all, the 25-year-old businessperson you may think is unable to make an irrevocable bequest or purchase a whole life insurance policy naming a charity as beneficiary may have made it big in the stock market or recently inherited a large sum that would allow him/her to make an outright contribution.

Although it's necessary to narrow your pool of major gift prospects in order to effectively manage a tracking system, always begin with the assumption that all prospects are capable of giving substantial gifts until proven otherwise.

Mine Diamonds in the Rough

Don't judge prospects by their looks, dress or environment. Diamonds in their natural state don't look at all like those you see in jewelry stores. It takes work, skill and polish to perfect them into gems.

It's the same with prospects. Sometimes their value is hard to see until you work with them and polish them to perfection.

Most veteran development pros can name at least one prospect who was a diamond in the rough, uninterested in the project, with no desire to give money. But months or even years of cultivation turned that rough prospect into a gem of a donor.

Learn to look beyond the shell and see a person's real value underneath and you'll soon be mining your own donor diamonds.

Assign Someone to Keep an Eye on the Big Picture

Regardless of the size of your development staff, one individual should be assigned responsibility for "managing" and tracking all major gift prospects. In many development shops, the researcher in charge of relationship management may fill this role to provide clear accountability and someone with his/her eye on the big picture. In addition, if the name of a new prospect is given, other staff and volunteers know who should receive it.

Assigning one individual as manager of major gifts, however, does not mean that person is responsible for the cultivation and solicitation of all prospects. Other staff and volunteers can be assigned to particular prospects based on any number of criteria: gift potential, regions, constituent type (individuals, businesses, foundations), etc.

Some key responsibilities of the major gifts manager include the following:

1. Compiling an ever-changing list of major gift prospects and donors. The size of this list may vary from organization to organization. Depending on your threshold of what is considered to be a major gift. For many nonprofit organizations, however, it's not uncommon to have a list of several dozen to thousands of prospects/donors.

2. Providing timely reports to staff involved with cultivation and solicitation activities.

3. Calling meetings to review names of prospects and donors and determining appropriate next steps, prospect strategy or meetings to rate and screen prospects in a group setting.

4. Managing the maintenance of prospect and donor information: call reports, profiles, correspondence, etc.

5. Monitoring all activities taking place with all major gift prospects.

6. Accepting referrals of potential donors and reviewing them in conjunction with others involved with major gifts activities.

7. Supporting those persons engaged in donor cultivation, solicitation and stewardship and keeping them apprised of any developments or useful information.

8. Evaluating progress being made toward individual and collective goals.

Keep Up Your Skills

Prospect research is an ever-changing field, where tools and technology can expand and alter the way you work on an almost-daily basis. To keep your skills and knowledge updated, check out the following organizations for continuing training, resources and other benefits.

Advancement Solutions Consulting Group

Association of Fundraising Professionals (AFP)

Association of Healthcare Philanthropy (AHP)

Association of Professional Researchers for Advancement (APRA)

Council for Advancement and Support of Education (CASE)

ePhilanthropy Foundation

The Center on Philanthropy at Indiana University - IUPUI

The Helen Brown Group, LLC

Calculate Value of Time Spent on Prospect Research

Does your organization track its return on investment (ROI) on prospect research? Could you, for example, state the percentage of new prospects identified by various referral sources? The percent of prospects converted at each stage of the fundraising cycle? The accuracy of different gift-rating mechanisms?

If not, help is on the way. Sally Boucher, longtime fundraiser and consultant at WealthEngine (Bethesda, MD), shares advice on calculating fundraising ROI and examples of fundraising metrics in action:

Where do nonprofits understand ROI and where do they not?

"Nonprofits are generally pretty good at calculating ROI for fundraising activities on a cost-per-dollar-raised basis. Attributing value to research functions, though, tends to be much more anecdotal. Because research doesn't directly bring in revenue, it can be hard to separate it from other major gift expenditures."

How difficult is it to start tracking the metrics needed to calculate fundraising ROI?

"The key to calculating ROI is having a workable prospect management system. I know not all organizations have one, but if you want to really assess fundraising activities, you need to look at end results, and that requires having a way to track prospects through the entirety of the funding cycle."

Are there metrics you feel are frequently overlooked or undervalued?

"Nonprofits are often good at tracking prospects identified, but sometimes fall short when it comes to conversion rates — looking at things like how prospects move through the fundraising cycle and where they are hung up in certain stages. Measuring time commitments — both how long prospects spend at any stage and how much time staff spend on given activities or areas — is crucial in evaluating the overall success of your operation."

What kinds of technology are needed to set up a solid system of prospect tracking?

"Most fundraising software comes with some sort of prospect management, but a lot can be done with a simple spreadsheet. Any organization can do it if they are willing to allocate someone to build a good system, take ownership in it and spend some time monitoring it."

What do nonprofits need to do (or not do) with the data they collect?

"There is no point collecting data if it's not going to be used, and used productively. Metrics are not a way to keep tabs on other departments or individuals, but a way to look at the system ... to determine where the problem areas — and the opportunity areas — are. The value of tracking metrics is that they provide a way for everyone to come together at the table, look at the data, and figure out what the best adjustment is."

Source: Sally Boucher, Consultant, WealthEngine, Mt. Pleasant, SC. E-mail: sboucher@wealthengine.com

This graph from WealthEngine (Mt. Pleasant, SC) shows one way to measure return on investment of time spent identifying major gift prospects.

Content not available in this edition

Glossary of Terms Used in Prospect Research

Analytics: Involves examining data to look for relationships and patterns to inform business understanding and decision making.

Annual Report: A voluntary report issued by a foundation or corporation that recaps its accomplishments for the year and provides financial data and descriptions of its grant making activities.

Bequest: A gift provided for in a person's will.

Capital Campaign: An intensive, organized fundraising effort to secure major gifts and pledges toward specific capital needs or projects (such as buildings, construction or equipment) within a finite time period (usually one or more years).

Case Statement: A document stating the most crucial financial needs of an organization.

Challenge Grant: Also called a matching grant, it is paid only if the organization is able to raise additional funds from other sources. Challenge grants are often used to stimulate giving from other donors.

Comprehensive Campaign: Similar to a capital campaign, these efforts encompass a broader range of needs, often including annual giving as well as facilities and endowment. These campaigns usually have larger overall goals than capital campaigns and extend over a longer period of years.

Contact Report (Call Report): The report is made when a move is made or a contact results in new or substantive information on an existing or potential donor.

Data Mining: The process of selecting, exploring and modeling large amounts of raw data to uncover previously unknown trends and patterns. This can help identify different types of potential prospects based on how they compare to known donors in your database.

Database Screening: A variety of vendors match your database records against information the vendor has on file. Some of this information may be individual-specific, such as stockholdings; some may be household specific, such as someone in the household owns a yacht; still others may be based on census data, such as the fact the individual lives in a wealthy area.

E-philanthropy: The use of the Internet for philanthropic purposes. Strategies include websites, electronic newsletters, e-mail communication and mechanisms for online donations.

Insider: The interpretation of insider varies from company to company but is generally those individuals considered to be in a policy-making position. You can usually count on the CEO, president and directors being classified as insiders. Other titles, such as executive vice president, may or may not be insiders. Owners of five percent or more of any one class of stock are also treated as insiders.

Online Databases: Online databases are electronic collections of information that can help you find answers about your prospects. There are thousands of online databases, most of them available to the public, with information ranging from directories of foundation grants or company information, to collections of full-text newspapers. Full-text databases can be useful for searching individual names that might not be the primary focus of an article and would not appear in an index or abstract.

Peer Screening: This is a process in which selected groups of people review lists of potential donors to help identify those best able to make large gifts. Consider peer screening if you need to increase your major gift pool or are planning to launch a capital campaign.

Prospect: In major gift terms, a prospect is an individual, foundation or corporation capable of making a significant gift to an organization.

Proxy Statements and 10Q/10K Filings: These filings are required of all public companies by the Securities and Exchange Commission. Items of interest to prospect researchers in the proxy statements include the five most highly paid officers, compensation and stock holdings of corporate insiders. The information in the 10K and 10Q may expand on the proxy statement and include detailed sales information.

Relationship Management: A focused process of prospect identification, research, clearance, cultivation, solicitation and recognition to achieve specific fundraising goals and to nurture enduring relationships with donors.

Stewardship: A process that conveys donor appreciation and enhances donor relationships.

990s and 990-PFs: The IRS requires all private foundations to file tax returns (990-PF forms) on an annual basis and to make these forms available to the public. The returns contain basic information including grant and trustee listings. This information can be useful for fundraisers who work with foundations, and the forms often include more detail than can be found in directories and databases.

Identify Essential Research Resources

Although essential prospect research tools for a large university may be quite different from those for a local youth agency, it's important to identify and access those basic research tools that can enhance your likelihood of securing major gifts no matter where you work. The costs for these resources are often competitive, however, some of them are priced for major libraries rather than small nonprofits. (Contact the vendors for current prices and other available resources.)

DIRECTORIES

- **Business Week's Company Insight Center** has information on more than 42,000 public and 322,000 private companies worldwide. You can find stock quotes and charts; news and press releases; financials and key competitors; research compensation figures; biographies; and board relationships of key company executives. Up-to-the-minute global sector and industry news is also available.

- **D&B's North American Million Dollar Database** provides information on approximately 1.6 million U.S. and Canadian leading public and private businesses. Company data includes industry information, employee numbers and annual sales, type of ownership, principal executives and biographies.

- **Foundation Directory Online** provides details available on more than 92,000 U.S. foundations and corporate donors, 1.3 million recent grants and more than 400,000 key decision makers, updated continually. Information is also available in books and on CDs.

- **GuideStar** provides free information (from 990 forms) on more than 1.5 million IRS-recognized nonprofit organizations. It also offers premium services with a fee-based subscription.

- **Hoover's Online** is a one-stop reference for business information on more than 24 million public and private companies. You can search their profile database for free information on companies, industries and executives. Subscription services offer additional data and search capabilities. They also produce several business handbooks in print format each year.

- **Marquis Who's Who** biographies are available in more than a dozen specialized print directories and an online database. They feature more than 1.4 million leaders and achievers from around the world, both past and present, and from every significant field of endeavor.

RESEARCH DATABASES

- **AlumniFinder**: An online tool to find lost alumni and other constituents, it also provides information on business executives, lets you screen for wealth and helps identify matching gift companies. Most areas are updated daily.

- **Canadian Revenue Agency**: Use this site to search their list of approximately 80,000 registered Canadian charities, including charities registered within the last 12 months.

- **DIALOG**: DIALOG has been around for years and provides online-based data from more than 15 terabytes of information in the areas of business, science, government, law, engineering and finance, among others.

- **Gale's Biography Resource Center**: This resource contains more than 435,000 biographies from more than 135 Gale reference sources, as well as full-text articles from nearly 300 magazines specifically chosen for their value to biographical research.

- **Harris Connect**: It helps you locate lost alumni, past members and other constituents using a variety of powerful search tools and databases. Services and products include directories, data cleaning services, NCOA, e-mail/phone number append, customized segmentation tools and predictive modeling.

- **KnowX.com**: This site provides access to a number of public record databases. KnowX's Executive Affiliation helps determine an executive's involvement with companies and relationships with other executives. Some searches are free, but there is always a fee to view results.

- **LexisNexis for Development Professionals**: This is a tool used to find and track background information on individual and corporate donors, and includes data such as contact information; property; aircraft and boat registrations; stocks; military personnel; professional licenses; and Social Security death records. Prices vary per user and organization type.

- **PRO Platinum/iWave**: Prospect Research Online (PRO) Platinum, by iWave Information Systems, is a subscription-based tool that helps identify and qualify individual, foundation and corporate giving prospects. Service includes a subscription to ZoomInfo.

continued on page 13

continued from page 12

- Telematch: Computerized U.S. and Canadian residential telephone number appending for residential or business phone numbers, it has more than 12 million residential phone numbers and more than 14 million business phone numbers.

- Yahoo! People Search: Yahoo! provides a free search database for mail and e-mail addresses and telephone numbers.

- ZoomInfo: Millions of executive biographies have been extracted from the Internet for this service, giving you access to profile information on more than 40 million people and 3.5 million companies. It includes cached biographies from 2001 and earlier, providing a source for past employment, which may not be available from someone's current online bio.

RESEARCH LINKS AND STARTING POINTS

- David Lamb's Prospect Research Page was one of the first to bring together links to essential websites that aid in researching prospects and donors. It is well annotated to help you pick the appropriate links.

- Search Systems provides access to more than 7,700 public records databases, searchable by U.S. nationwide, by state, and by Canadian and worldwide resources. It includes links to real estate records, professional directories, death records, bank locators, etc.

- The University of Southern California's research department has pulled together a useful set of resources with an especially strong international section.

- The University of Virginia has categorized its vast collection of links into biographical, salary, stock, business, etc. It is well organized and fairly comprehensive.

- Northwestern University's site a treasure trove of research links, including sections on patents, real estate, mergers/acquisitions and government links.

BIOGRAPHIES & GENEALOGY SITES

- Ancestry.com allows searches of more than five billion names in more than 25,000 databases, including the Social Security Death Index (with birth, marriage, divorce and death dates), the U.S. Census Collection and historical newspapers. Some of the services require a paid subscription.

- Cyndi's List has more than 260,000 links to genealogy sites, lists, libraries and history centers.

SOCIAL MEDIA SITES

- Facebook, with hundreds of millions of users, is the largest social media space on line. Users determine how much of their profile to share public, so the depth of information you find on prospects will vary.

- LinkedIn is focused on promoting professional connections. Offers valuable search functions with expanded access through paid subscription.

- Twitter is a site that lets you track hot topics and interests of your prospects through their posts of 140 characters or less.

- Doctor Finder is a service of the American Medical Association and provides information on physicians in the U.S., searchable by name or specialty.

- Martindale-Hubbell's Lawyer Locator is a searchable directory of more than one million attorneys and law firms in more than 160 countries.

- Forbes has lists of people and companies from celebrities to the just plain rich. You can search the database by different criteria. It includes very brief snapshots and estimated worth projections.

NEWS SOURCES

- American City Business Journals links to more than 40 business newspapers and their archives searchable individually or as a group. You can also sign up for daily e-mails of top national headlines.

- CEO Express has links to daily newspapers, business news and magazines, newswires, tech magazines, health sites, international news and business research links.

- Newspapers.com links to publications around the world, including college newspapers and business journals.

continued on page 14

continued from page 13

INTERNATIONAL RESOURCES

- The Sunday Times has a Rich List area and a business section with Top 100 lists, Movers and Shakers articles and other items focused on the United Kingdom and Europe.
- The Search Engine Colossus is an international directory of search engines with links to information on more than 351 countries and territories.
- globalEDGE's Resource Desk has a rich collection, including links to periodicals, stock exchanges, banks, company directories and an international business glossary.

FUNDRAISING DATABASES

- Blackbaud offers several fundraising database products to meet the needs of advancement shops small and large, including The Raiser's Edge.,
- Ellucian combines SGHE and Datatel to offer several fundraising solutions including Advance, Banner and Colleague Advancement.

OTHER RESOURCES

Regardless of your budget's size, it's always helpful to find information which is free or fairly inexpensive. Fortunately, there are many sources which are relatively easy to obtain. Most of them require only a letter or phone call, and some of them may be found nearby.

- **College, university and public libraries** are probably the best free sources of information. Their collections often include many of the basic reference sources, such as *Who's Who, Dun & Bradstreet's Million Dollar Database*, the Foundation Center directories, etc. In addition, a number of the larger libraries have online searching stations to make your job much easier. The reference librarians who work there can point you in the right direction and will sometimes do the searches for you.
- Various **professional associations**, such as the Council for Advancement and Support of Education (CASE), the Association of Fundraising Professionals (AFP), the Association of Professional Researchers for Advancement (APRA), and the Association for Healthcare Philanthropy (AHP) have resource centers and librarians you can access by phone, online or by e-mail. Their information is generally free or low-cost to members.
- The **state attorney general and the secretary of state** are good sources for information on foundations and corporations, although some offices (and their websites) are more helpful than others. The corporation/securities division of the state will have information on local private companies which may be difficult to find elsewhere.
- **City and state chambers of commerce** and **Better Business Bureaus** may also have information on local businesses, including directories and mailing lists for various types of companies. Although there is usually a charge for the directories, they are generally fairly inexpensive. If your organization is a member of the local chamber, make sure you sign up to get a copy of their monthly newsletter. It will often include good information on area companies and executives.
- Bentz Whaley Flessner, a fundraising consultant group, offers a free annual publication entitled *Bibliography: A Guide to Development Research Resources*. It includes listings of various types of resources for use in fundraising and prospect research, in addition to sections on topics such as data mining, information support systems and sample prospect profiles.
- Ask friendly (and generous) constituent members to donate resources such as **professional association directories, country club lists and social registers.**
- Another good resource is **honor rolls from other nonprofits.** You can use these to discover giving interests of donors you have in common and to find new prospects.
- Don't underestimate these internal resources: **historical files, campaign lists, event attendance lists, donor lists, members (past/present), current/former board members, current/past employees and past surveys.**

Subscribing to E-mail List Software

LISTSERVs or list servers are distribution lists which bring together people for discussions on various topics through message postings that are sent to and from the subscribers. The owners and sites occasionally change, so you may need to verify the subscription information if you have problems signing on to them. Here are some of the many lists that are relevant to fundraising.

- **ADVANCE-L:** A CASE-owned list for senior advancement professionals. To subscribe, go to http://list.case.org/cgi-bin/wa.exe?A0=Advance-L and follow the instructions.
- **CANADA-PRSPCT-L:** Provides a forum for the discussion of prospect research issues from a Canadian perspective. To subscribe, go to www.groups.yahoo.com/group/CANADA-PRSPCT-L.
- **CFRNET:** Focuses on corporate and foundation relations issues in fundraising. To subscribe, go to http://stenosis.wustl.edu/cgi-bin/lyris.pl?join=cfrnet
- **CHARITY CHANNEL:** Charity Channel maintains many useful Listservs on various topics. You must be a member to sign up for many of them, including:
- **CFRESEARCH:** Focuses on corporate and foundation prospect research.
- **GRANTS:** Focuses on all aspects of grants and foundations.

- **STEWARDSHIPLIST:** For use by stewardship and donor relations professionals.
- **FUNDLIST:** Operates as a general fundraising discussion group. To subscribe, go to www.fundlist.info/
- **FUNDSVCS:** List for advancement services and gift processing professionals. To subscribe, go to http://listserv.fundsvcs.org/cgi-bin/wa?SUBED1=fundsvcs&A=1
- **GIFT-PL:** A listserv for use by planned giving officers. To subscribe, go to https://listserv.iupui.edu/cgi-bin/wa-iupui.exe?SUBED1=GIFT-PL&A=1
- **PROSPECT- DMM:** A discussion group for development professionals involved or interested in data mining and modeling, particularly as such concepts may be applied to major gifts. To subscribe, go to https://mailman.mit.edu/mailman/listinfo/prospect-dmm
- **PRSPCT-L:** The prospect research discussion list is managed by APRA (Association of Professional Researchers for Advancement). To subscribe, go to http://listserv.apra-prspct-l.org/wa.exe?A0=PRSPCT-L

Perform Searches on the Internet

The Internet is not indexed in any standard manner, so finding specific information can seem difficult. Search engines are great tools, but they often return thousands of hits (if not hundreds of thousands), and the results can be overwhelming.

No matter what search engine you utilize, you must first have a clear understanding of how to prepare your search. Here are some helpful tips in creating your search terms for the best results:

- Search engines are not case sensitive (e.g., you don't need to type any capital letters).
- Perform the same search on several search engines to increase your results.
- BASIC SEARCH — john adams retrieves anything with either "john" or "adams"
- EXACT PHRASE — "john q. adams" (with quotes) retrieves the name only with the middle initial, and in that order.
- REQUIRED WORDS — john AND adams or john +adams (with space before + symbol) retrieves listings

with both "john" and "adams" (but not necessarily together as "john adams").
- EXCLUDED WORDS — john NOT adams or john - adams (with space before - symbol) lists sites with "john" but not "adams" on them. Some search engines prefer AND NOT (two words) or ANDNOT (one word) rather than just NOT, so you may need to experiment.
- MULTIPLE WORDS — You could also use parentheses to further refine a search. john NOT (adams OR hancock) would exclude "adams" and "hancock" from any listings.
- WILDCARDS — The asterisk (*) character can help you search when you're not sure of a word's spelling or if a term is plural. john* adam* will return listings with "john" or "johnny" or "adam" or "adams" or any combination. Some sites support two (2) wildcards. The asterisk(*) is used to replace multiple characters and the percent (%) symbol is used to replace only one character. jo%n retrieves any listings with "john" or "joan" in them.

Hiring Research Staff

A critical aspect of an effective research operation lies in hiring a knowledgeable and productive staff. You can have all the resources at your disposal, but you need staff members who are trained to use them to be truly successful. Whether you are recruiting new staff or moving current employees into research positions, you should consider the following key factors in the process.

Define your needs. These will determine some of the basic skills you need to establish as requirements in your position description.

- Are you looking for someone who will produce profiles and reports in a back-room atmosphere or do you need someone who can interact with front-line staff?
- Decide if your researcher will be responsible for maintaining your computer database and files, and whether or not you need someone who can generate reports from that system.
- Do the donor relations and stewardship functions belong to the research area or do you have other staff members handling these duties?
- What about prospect management and tracking and fundraising analytics? Will your researcher be dealing with these systems, and if so, what level of expertise is needed in this area? The APRA Skills Sets can help you establish job descriptions for your research positions. Contact APRA for more information.

Define your budget. The staff size and resource allocations will vary based on your organization and campaign stage.

- Salaries and professional development costs will probably take up the largest percentage of your budget for this area. Unless they are serving in a purely clerical function, researchers should be paid at the same level as front-line fundraisers with equal experience, and should have similar titles.
- Consider whether or not your circumstances will warrant hiring additional researchers or clerical staff. You generally will want to consider increasing your staff when you are gearing up for a campaign, adding front-line fundraisers or creating new programs. The research support structure should grow as the rest of the organization grows.

Define your research stage. The type of research you need will determine the qualifications you should seek in your researchers.

- Researchers can help you locate and prioritize prospects on the front end of the campaign, manage the prospects during the campaign and analyze the results at the end of the campaign.
- Do you want your researchers to be proactive in discovering new prospects or do you want them to focus on analyzing the prospects you already know?
- Do you have special projects or programs which need in-depth research or analysis? Are you planning to purchase database screening services or hold peer screening sessions?

Identify key characteristics. Although each organization will have its own set of personnel requirements, successful and productive researchers often have similar characteristics.

- Researchers should have strong interpersonal and written communication skills.
- Look for good problem solvers who can analyze and synthesize data into meaningful and useful information.
- They should be computer literate and able to type.
- Familiarity with the Internet, library resources and online services is often required, in addition to basic research skills.
- Productive researchers usually are aided by curiosity, intelligence and a good sense of humor, and they should be good team leaders.

Decide on the best employment status. Budget and research needs will help determine how the researchers are hired.

- Full-time researchers offer the best support, and they can develop proactive, big picture views of your prospects. They are familiar with the organization and the prospects, and work as part of the team.
- If you don't have the budget resources or research demands, part-time staff can provide useful services by handling special projects or limited profile requests.
- Freelance and contract researchers generally charge by the hour or by the profile, in addition to passing on any costs they incur. This can be expensive in the long run if you have a large number of profiles, but can be effective for short-term projects or small groups of prospects.

Documentation and Training Procedures

Whether you have staff or volunteer turnover, you are implementing a new program, or you have a new computer system to install, training and documentation are vital to a smooth-running operation. These tips and guidelines should help you establish or fine-tune procedures for your organization.

Documentation
- In-house training should include a manual or documentation to accompany it.
- Remember to separate policies from procedures. (Policies are the why; procedures represent the how-to.)
- Set up the manual so you can distribute different parts to different users based on their functions and the structure of your organization. Detailed data entry procedures need to be given only to the staff or volunteers who will be performing those duties. Likewise, policies which affect staff may not apply to volunteers. Determine the audience and define your documentation based on their varying needs.
- If you are creating a new manual, set deadlines for completing each section. Make it easy to update. Keep it short, but allow for additions as they are needed.
- Policies and procedures should be defined through a collaborative effort. Set up a task force or committee if necessary, but remember to have procedures written by someone familiar with the processes.
- The person writing the documentation should be able to communicate to users effectively.
- Some of the information in a manual might include: a confidentiality policy, a glossary of terminology, report formats and how to read them, instructions for using e-mail and telephone systems, examples of forms, dress codes, organization charts and directories, how to access information from files and the computer system, and step-by-step instructions for data entry.

Training
Once your documentation has been set up, a training method needs to be defined.

- Determine the best format for training sessions based on the types of information, your organization's resources, and the needs of the people involved. Various methods include using written workbooks, audio, videos, hands-on computer examples, or some combination of these.
- Set up a training schedule. Decide how many sessions will be needed and the appropriate length of each one. Keep in mind the complexity of the information being provided and how much your audience can realistically absorb. This will help to determine the effectiveness of longer sessions as opposed to several shorter meetings.
- Give trainees something to take with them as a practice tool and have them return for a follow-up session to measure their understanding and address further questions.
- Set up a help desk or designate specific individuals with responsibility for answering questions on procedures and policies.
- Be sure that training is ongoing and reflects changes taking place within your organization.

Sample Table of Contents
From a Training Manual

Table of Contents

Introduction
    Campaign Management Information
        Flow...to Information Base
    Campaign Management Information
        Flow...from Information Base
    Prospect Classifications
    Prospect Classification Process

Information Input Screens
    Visual Clues to Reading Screens
    Accessing System
    Signing off System
    Entering Call Reports

Reports
    Donor Profile (Individuals example)
    Donor Profile (Organizations example)
    Prospect Assignment Request
    Call Report
    Scheduled Next Steps Report
    Activity Report
    Proposal Status Report
    Proposal Summary Report

Tables
    Gift Tender Codes
    Gift Type Codes
    Lifestyle Categories
    Solicitation Status Codes

Glossary
Index

Building Strong Relationships With Fundraisers

One of the challenges of prospect research can be stepping back from our quest for information in order to build relationships with the gift officers we serve. These relationships, however, have as much to do with a successful career in research as does knowing where to find the right information.

Here are some ideas to help you expand and develop your relationships with gift officers.

- **Reach out.** Playing offense can help you stay a step ahead. Find out what your gift officer's priorities are for the month, quarter or year. Then think of ways you can help him achieve his goals.

- **Ask for clarification.** Often a gift officer has something very particular in mind when she asks for research. When appropriate, ask questions to gain a better understanding of what information she wants most. These sorts of clues can help you find better information, narrow your focus and show you are committed to providing what the gift officer needs. All of this, in turn, means you provide a better product, and everyone is happier!

- **Stay abreast of travel plans and prospect visits.** Finding a way to stay tuned in to your gift officer's plans will help you to be proactive. If he is travelling to another city, you could suggest a list of prospects he might want to call. If he has a meeting with Mr. Smith, you could do a quick search to see if there has been any news on Mr. Smith recently.

- **Share relevant news stories or articles.** Finding news on prospects is extremely helpful to gift officers — knowing the good, the bad and the ugly helps them to plan strategies for cultivation and solicitation. Even if a gift officer has already seen an article, she will be impressed that you picked up on the connection.

- **Choose your communication method wisely.** E-mail seems to rule our world, especially for those of us who are constantly searching for information online. Picking up the phone can be useful when a complex question needs answering or when it is time for negotiating. Always seek out opportunities for occasional face-to-face contact, too. Finding a balance of these three communication methods will help to keep communication flowing.

Source: Caroline Rossini, Research Analyst, Vanderbilt University. E-mail: Caroline.rossini@vanderbilt.edu

Prospect Research Fundamentals: Proven Methods to Help Charities Realize More Major Gifts, Fourth Edition.
Edited by Elizabeth Dollhopf-Brown.
© 2012 Stevenson, Inc. Published 2012 by Stevenson, Inc.

The future success of your program depends upon your ability to identify prospects who possess both the financial ability and the proclivity to invest in your cause, as well as your ability to replenish the prospect pool and continue to expand your donor base.

Take a Four-sided Approach to Prospect Identification

Identifying prospects may feel like looking for a needle in a haystack. Many organizations have entire research teams dedicated to the task; others rely largely on the luck of the draw. Whatever your organization's size or capacity, here are four lenses experts in the philanthropic fundraising field agree will help you to identify prospects who will make worthwhile additions to your donor pool:

1. **Financial viability**. It's not enough to know a donor is wealthy. In today's economy, it's important to know what type of wealth your prospect has. A little bit of research and time with a calculator can tell you a donor's approximate financial worth: work history can guide you to approximate salary, while a home address can give you an idea of property value. Even resources such as family obituaries can help you understand how much a donor's family may have. How does the prospect spend leisure time? Does he/she have stocks? How are those stocks doing? Gauge giving capacity by looking at past philanthropy to other organizations. By simply combing public records, you can educate your gift officers as to the realistic feasibility of a gift. This keeps you from wasting the time and resources of both you and your prospect.

2. **Connection to your organization.** For many gift officers, organizational affiliation is the first step in connecting with a potential donor. Experts say that merely relying on your organization's reach can limit your scope. By exploring a potential prospect's background, you may unearth a less obvious connection to your organization or your organization's mission: maybe she took a summer program at your university as a child; maybe he has a grandchild with the same learning disability for which your organization has developed a new treatment. However small the connection may seem initially, it could be the key to a long-lasting and lucrative relationship with a new donor. You won't know the depth of that connection until you plumb it.

3. **Philanthropy.** As mentioned above, a donor's philanthropic activity can offer clues to financial solvency. Past giving can also help identify something more difficult to quantify: a donor's interest in helping others, and the way(s) in which he/she goes about doing so. Just because a donor gives to an organization similar to yours doesn't mean he/she wouldn't also be interested in giving to your cause. Or maybe your organization offers something (a research focus or aspect of patient care, for example) that the donor's current charity does not. The same argument holds true if the prospect gives to organizations with very different missions than your own. Just because they support such causes doesn't mean they'll say no to your request.

4. **Demographic.** Persons with the capacity to give may be more or less likely to do so depending on where they are in their lives and careers. For instance, if your organization engages in cutting-edge or experimental research, you may have more success attracting younger donors more willing to invest in such an untested effort than retired donors, who may prefer giving to well-known organizations rooted in tradition. It is a more efficient use of your fundraisers' energy to match donors with projects more likely to meet their social and financial demographic.

Useful Rule of Thumb

■ In any major gifts effort, no fewer than 100 top prospects should be identified to build a strong program. What you set as a minimum major gift (e.g., $10,000; $50,000 or $100,000) will help to determine the collective potential that exists. Developing strategic involvement plans with these top 100-plus prospects is vital to an organization's success in securing major gifts.

Prospect Identification Key to Early Success in Major Campaign

Nine months into the silent phase of the comprehensive campaign for Ripon College (Ripon, WI), college representatives announced they had already secured $9.5 million of their $50 million working goal. And since then, they have secured three additional seven-figure commitments.

Vice President for Advancement Wayne Webster says he and his colleagues hoped to raise 40 percent of their working campaign total during the two-year silent phase, which launched July 1, 2010.

Webster says plans are to approach 100 donors and prospective donors during the silent phase to secure early leadership gifts. College officials chose the 100 based on a combination of capacity to give, positions of leadership in relation to the college, affinity for Ripon and past record of giving.

Those 100 top prospects represent 8.33 percent of the larger pool of 1,200 rated major gift prospects already identified for the actual campaign, says Webster. He notes, college officials anticipate they will need 1,500 major gift prospects to meet the goal.

To identify the 300 additional prospects, he says, college officials are:

✓ Running names of selected alumni, parents and friends through wealth search engines to identify prospective donors whose past giving history hasn't identified them as such.

✓ Asking for recommendations from currently engaged prospects and donors.

✓ Using a peer screening tool to identify additional major gift prospects by asking persons close to the campaign to review names of alumni who graduated two years before or after they did, as well as alumni, parents and friends from all eras who live in their geographic area.

Webster says the silent campaign is also buoyed by Ripon's long-standing tradition of carefully stewarding resources to maximize their impact on students and faculty. "A tremendous amount of our resources goes toward instruction and student aid. We have very little overhead, and our donors know that their gifts directly impact our faculty and students," he says. "Being able to show our donors the outcomes and beneficiaries of their commitments by showcasing our tremendous faculty and students makes a tremendous impact as well."

He says they educate current and potential donors of their gifts' impact through annual endowment performance reports, thank-you notes from students, scholarship donor recognition dinners, and by having the president personally solicit and thank leadership donors.

Source: Wayne P. Webster, Vice President for Advancement, Ripon College, Ripon, WI. E-mail: WebsterW@ripon.edu

Key Metrics Measure Campaign Silent Phase

Ripon College (Ripon, WI) just completed a two-year silent phase of a $50 million capital campaign. Vice President for Advancement Wayne Webster cites three key metrics to watch in a capital campaign's silent phase:

1. Number of visits by gift officers to ensure cultivation of both silent- and public-phase prospect pools.

2. Number of prospective donors for each category within the campaign giving period (generally requires three to four prospects for each gift needed).

3. Dollars coming in and from whom. Do you have the pipeline needed to raise the remaining campaign total once you go public?

Make Time to Review Old Prospect Files

Have you ever been given the name of a potentially fantastic gift prospect only to later find out the person's name was already in your files but no one had ever followed up on connecting with him/her?

Whether you've just taken on a new position or been in your current position forever, don't underestimate the value of reviewing existing files in your quest to uncover sleeping giants. Many times files hold a wealth of names and information that never received the proper attention and follow-up they deserved.

Make a point to methodically go through all files in an effort to identify and prioritize major gift prospects.

Mine Your Existing Database for Prospects, Then Prioritize

Since the key to building a major donor program is creating and maintaining relationships, look first to your database of supporters for potential major gifts, says Sandra G. Ehrlich, director of fund development services at Zielinski Companies (St. Louis, MO).

According to industry statistics, approximately 4 to 5 percent of the current donors in your database have the ability to make a major gift, says Ehrlich. For example, if your database contains 5,000 names, it should contain 150 to 200 potential major donors.

"Use your database to determine how many individuals are giving at a significant level," she says. "Begin by running a report of donors who have made a $1,000 single gift. If you find 10,000 donors, you'll need to revise your criteria. If you find 100, you are in the ballpark. If you find only two, drop the baseline to $500 and go from there."

After determining your baseline and criteria for a major donor, separate major donors and prospects into meaningful and manageable segments, she says: "Zielinski Companies recommends creating tiers of major donors and prospects to care for each donor as personally as you can, while staying focused on those donors who will likely give the majority of funds in any given campaign or year."

Tier 1 donors are your top donors who rate high in capability and willingness in a consistent and strategic manner.

Tier 2 donors may be high in capacity or willingness, but likely not both.

Tier 3 prospects are those with whom you have some connection, are known to have capacity, but haven't yet developed a deep knowledge of or interest in your organization.

Rank your major donors on their proximity to the gift, says Ehrlich, by asking:

- How close are they to giving?
- Have you been in touch with them recently?
- Have they been in touch with you recently?
- Have they hinted or stated that an outright gift might be coming?
- Do you know them well enough?
- Do you feel comfortable that you might receive a gift on the next call?

"Major donors are often rated initially on a two-part scale: willingness and capability," she says. "Willingness refers to a donor's connection to your organization and his or her level of interest and commitment to support the difference you are making in the community. Capability refers to a donor's financial capacity to support your organization."

Once you finish ranking your major donors, consider the capacity of your staff to manage those prospects, says Ehrlich:

"A full-time major gifts officer can likely handle between 50 and 100 of your Tier 1 donors. Another 200 to 300 donors may fit into the Tier 2 segment. When functioning optimally, your nonprofit will be in touch in a meaningful way with all three tiers at least once a month. For Tier 1 donors and prospects, you'll need to create individualized strategies based on your knowledge of those individuals. For Tiers 2 and 3, you'll create group strategies that are as personalized as possible."

Source: Sandra G. Ehrlich, Director, Fund Development Services, Zielinski Companies, St. Louis, MO. E-mail: sehrlich@zielinskico.com

Building a Mailing List From Scratch

Whether you are expanding an established mailing list or starting from scratch, it's important to selectively build your list if you hope to cultivate new and larger gifts.

Begin expanding your list by adding names of those who visit your organization.

- Place a guest book in key locations that are frequented by visitors to your organization.
- Have a fish bowl available for business cards — include a monthly drawing for an item with your nonprofit's logo on it.
- Include a return postcard in mailings that invites new names to be added to your mailing list.

- Add all current, past and potential vendors.
- Review names of top donors to other organizations, and add appropriate names to your list.
- Include current and retired employees.
- Add current as well as past board members.
- Don't forget the obvious — those who have benefited from your services (and perhaps relatives of former customers).
- Include active and past volunteers.
- Selectively add residents of exclusive ZIP codes who might be potential constituents.
- Expand your list of major businesses and foundations.
- Buy mailing lists of prospects based on similar interests as the target market for your organization.

Reeher Platform Helps Find New Prospects, Increase Giving

Gift prospecting can sometimes feel like searching for a needle in a haystack. You know the right donors are out there, you just don't have the tools to find them.

When Temple University wanted to enhance its prospect portfolios, they got some help by joining the Reeher Platform, the first shared management system dedicated to higher-education fundraising. According to Reeher, the platform can help colleges and universities find up to 40 percent of new best-prospect donors and uncover nearly 30 percent of wasted fundraising time, money and energy.

"It's bridging the gap between what organizations know and what they can do with that data," says Andy Reeher, the president and CEO.

Because the platform is Web-based, implementation can start very quickly, and the shared aspect of it allows for a more dynamic product, according to David Unruh, vice president for institutional advancement at Temple.

"We all benefit from suggestions and upgrades other institutions make, so it doesn't become a static platform," says Unruh. "It's regularly being changed, enhanced and getting better, whereas other platforms you sort of buy them and you implement them and they're very costly to update, or you have to wait for annual or biannual updates instead of a

constant stream of enhancements and recommendations."

The University of Cincinnati has been a part of the platform for five years, and Reeher says he has seen UC's donations increase from $65 million a year to over $100 million a year during that time. He has also seen their principal-gift prospects, or those rated at being able to donate $1 million a year, increase from 72 to 450.

Although Temple has only been using the platform for two months, Unruh says he is very pleased with the results. "This really gives us the flexibility to make more informed decisions and be thoughtful about where we're applying resources and time. Ideally, we are taking an existing budget allocation and using it more effectively. We are getting greater results, even in the absence of increased budget," says Unruh.

Reeher says the cost of the platform is tiered and based on the size of the institution and how much money it raises, but it works out to be the same as the cost of a full-time employee, or possibly two depending on the organization.

Sources: Andy Reeher, President and CEO, Reeher LLC, St. Paul, MN. E-mail: info@reeher.net. David Unruh, Senior Vice President for Institutional Advancement, Temple University, Philadelphia, PA. E-mail: david.unruh@temple.edu

Benefits of Obituary Review

Reviewing obituaries is a fairly straightforward element of prospect research.

Depending on the scope of your constituency, you may need to include several regional papers along with your local ones. You may not need a subscription, as most newspapers now post obituaries online. Some services provide automated e-mail alerts to send obituaries to you by e-mail.

Here are seven reasons for development officers to keep an eye on obituaries:

1. To keep your donor list updated by checking names against your database. Marking records inactive saves on postage and helps avoid awkward situations with the deceased's family.

2. To send condolence letters to surviving members is a thoughtful act of stewardship, especially with major donors and prospects. Consider having high-level staff make a memorial gift to your cause to show the family how highly you regarded the person.

3. To discover family relationships and other valuable information to locate new prospects and learn more about current donors, such as relatives' names, locations and occupations.

4. If your organization is listed as a memorial recipient, you and your staff can prepare to receive gifts, draft acknowledgment letters or create a named endowment or other special fund.

5. Memorial listings, while often reflecting the deceased's wishes, can help identify surviving relatives' philanthropic interests and lead named organizations to new sources of gifts.

6. If you keep track of persons who have included your nonprofit in their wills, obituaries can trigger procedures for your planned giving staff. While estates may need to go through probate first, death notices can give you an idea of when to expect contributions.

7. Healthcare providers may get an added bonus if the family includes acknowledgment listings in obituaries. Something as simple as "the family wishes to thank St. Mary's Hospital for the capable and sensitive care they provided" may offer positive public relations for the nonprofit.

Although treating the deceased with respect is the first and foremost principle to follow, do not underestimate the value of information to be found in obituaries.

Get Employees Involved With Referrals

Looking for new ways to identify prospects capable of making $25,000-and-above or other significant gifts? Go to your fellow employees for guidance.

Your charity's employees have a vested interest in wanting your organization to do well financially, so it makes perfect sense to seek their help. Begin by simply asking them for names of persons they know who are capable of making a major gift. The level of major gift will depend on your individual organization.

Let them know they can do a little or a lot — from sharing names in confidence to making introductions or even being a part of the solicitation process.

Distribute forms similar to the one shown below at least twice a year so employees know you're on the lookout for major gift prospects. And whenever an employee shares a name, follow up immediately to thank him/her and discuss next steps (the employee's possible level of involvement, more details about the prospect, etc.).

Subscribe to Newspapers to Identify Major Gift Prospects

If your organization is working to identify new major gift prospects — and what nonprofit isn't? — consider subscribing to the local newspaper, many of which now offer digital content.

While some local newspapers are challenged by the changing times, area news outlets will keep you up-to-date on important local happenings like business transactions, social events and philanthropic gifts, and newspapers will convey far more information per minute of time spent on them than other media like television or radio.

Even if you only have time to scan headlines, local newspapers are a resource no major gift officer should ignore.

Dear fellow employees of [name of nonprofit]: We could use your help!

Part of our ability to secure major gifts depends on our ability to identify individuals, organizations, clubs and businesses capable of making such gifts — gifts that add to our endowment, underwrite costs of existing and new programs; and help us purchase needed equipment and renovate facilities.

Once those prospects have been identified, we will work to interest and involve them in the life of [name of nonprofit]. That involvement will eventually result in significant investments in [name of nonprofit].

You can really help our efforts by sharing (in confidence) names of persons you know who are capable of making gifts of $25,000 or more [or level your individual charity deems as major gift level]. When you share one or more names, a representative from our office will contact you to discuss the name(s) and your level of interest in being involved in contacting and/or cultivating those listed. But know that you may choose the level of involvement — from sitting in on direct solicitation efforts, to simply sharing the name with us.

Please compete this form as names come to mind and return it to our office. (Additional forms can be supplied as needed.)

Thank you for your help!

Your Name & Department _____

1. Prospect _____
   Address _____
   Occupation _____
   Your relationship to prospect _____
   Source of wealth (business, inheritance, etc.) _____

2. Prospect _____
   Address _____
   Occupation _____
   Your relationship to prospect _____
   Source of wealth (business, inheritance, etc.) _____

3. Prospect _____
   Address _____
   Occupation _____
   Your relationship to this individual/business _____
   Source of wealth (business, inheritance, etc.) _____

Keep Adding to Your Prospect List

When someone shares the name of a new prospect, either intentionally or unintentionally, what becomes of it? Do you write the name down and take additional notes? Do you add them to your database? Do you see that some form of action takes place with regard to follow-up?

Your management system should include a method for garnering new names of potential donors and ensuring appropriate follow-up that either moves the prospect into your tracking cycle of research, introduction, cultivation, solicitation and stewardship, or eliminates the prospect from further consideration.

Encourage staff, volunteers and board members to become sensitive to names of individuals, businesses or foundations that might have gift potential. Develop a referral card that insiders can use to record and share names of donor hopefuls.

When you secure new names, or referrals are given to you, record them in your database and run a new prospect considerations report that calls for action to be taken within a specific time frame with clear objectives in mind.

Discuss the report at regular staff meetings to be sure appropriate follow-up is being taken and to determine next steps for each of the new prospects.

New Prospect Considerations Report

NAME	REFERRED BY	REFERRAL DATE	ASSIGNED TO	RATIONALE FOR CONSIDERATION	ACTION TAKEN	BY

Research Strategies Anyone Can Use

It may sometimes seem like you need to have access to a lot of expensive resources and dozens of staff members to accomplish any meaningful research, but that isn't true.

The following ideas prove that there are many alternatives and strategies.

❑ Network with current donors to review and rate prospects.
❑ Ask board members for background information on major donor prospects.
❑ Save newspaper clippings and sign up for e-mail alerts on businesses, individuals and foundations of interest.
❑ Review property databases and plat maps to determine who owns real estate in your area.
❑ Read obituaries and wedding announcements for family information and honor/memorial possibilities.
❑ Conduct phone calls and/or personal visits with anyone who has contact with your agency.
❑ Complete standardized contact reports following visits to compile a historical file.

❑ Secure a state bank directory listing boards of directors for each institution.
❑ Obtain personal referrals of prospects from board members and key volunteers.
❑ Coordinate focus group meetings to collectively discuss key prospects.
❑ Establish advisory committees in other communities to help identify local wealth.
❑ Review other agencies' lists of contributors.
❑ Review community and regional business journals, as well as company annual reports and chamber of commerce publications that provide news of employee promotions, business expansions and who's who profiles.
❑ Meet with your employees to review your organization's current and former customers and identify those with significant resources.
❑ Make brief questionnaires that ask individuals for their opinions on matters relating to your organization.

Board Candidate Application Screens Prospects

Staff at the Arts & Business Council of Greater Phoenix (Phoenix, AZ) use a board candidate application as part of its board member recruitment and screening process.

"Since we developed a more targeted board recruitment process, more board members are taking their job seriously and going out and recruiting board members," says Debra M. Paine, executive director. "A nonprofit is a business. If you don't treat it like a business, you're not going to be successful."

The application gathers the following information about each candidate:

❑ Professional experience for the past five to 10 years.

❑ Community, volunteer, and leadership activities for the past five to 10 years and why they found them rewarding.

❑ Strengths the prospect can bring to the board.

❑ The prospect's interest in the arts as well as other special interests.

❑ The prospect's professional business expertise (e.g., marketing/public relations, financial, legal, etc.).

The organization's board development committee reviews applications. Paine and the chair of the board development committee interview candidates over lunch.

"I participate in the interviews because that way they get to know me and how I operate as well," says Paine. "During the interview we ask the candidate about their interest in the arts, and the board chair shares his experience on the board.

We also explain their fiduciary responsibility, which includes the requirement that they give or get a minimum of $2,500 each year. However, they must give a personal contribution as part of that requirement. If they don't give, how can they ask others to give? It is an opportunity for board candidates to vet us as well as us to vet them and to learn more about their responsibilities."

Other tools that the Arts & Business Council of Greater Phoenix uses to recruit and select board candidates include:

✓ **A board inventory sheet** that lists the type of board members they currently have on the board and which they are seeking. The sheet includes age, gender, ethnicity, geographical distribution, expertise and type of community member each represents (arts, business, large or small company or self-employed, etc.).

✓ **A board affirmation agreement** that board members sign when they join the board which affirms their commitment to the organization's mission, to their legal and fiduciary responsibilities, and to the council's success.

✓ **A board term grid list** that lists current board members, the date they were elected, when their term ends, and in which category they fit, (e.g., technology, marketing, insurance, public relations/marketing, etc.).

Source: Debra M. Paine, Executive Director, Arts & Business Council of Greater Phoenix, Phoenix, AZ.
E-mail: dpaine@artsbusinessphoenix.org

Four Steps to Fundraising Analytics Success

Today's researchers often talk about analytics. At a basic level, analytics involves examining data to look for relationships and patterns to inform business understanding and decision making. It broadly includes descriptive statistics, mapping analysis, predictive modeling and more. Analysis in fundraising helps improve fundraising efficiency, validate hunches, and point to new opportunities or areas of concern. Many vendors are happy to help you with big projects, such as predictive modeling, but an analytical mindset can be applied to common fundraising situations, too. Analysis often includes the following steps for success:

1. **Start with a business question** — listen for why questions when you meet with your organization's managers. Analysis opportunities often stem from curiosity about the causes and influences of fundraising activity. For example, when looking at the pattern of gifts received, a manager may wonder why online giving spiked last week.

2. **Gather your data** — To explore the question, you need to gather all of the information that may be helpful.

Think about what you have that is accessible, relevant and current. You may need to clean up data (like correcting misspellings), but remember that your data set does not have to be perfect to be helpful for analysis. In our example, you may want to look at all of the gift data from last week and the schedule and content of all recent direct marketing materials, in print and online.

3. **Analyze!** — apply your tools to the data you gathered, starting with your thoughtful brain! Software products, like Excel, Tableau, SPSS, and MapPoint, may help reveal patterns in the details. You may find it helpful to bounce your initial findings off a colleague as you test your ideas. In our case, you might look at the gift data in Excel, review gifts by solicitation source and find that most came from an e-newsletter sent earlier in the month.

4. **Share your findings** — reporting back is an important step in analytics. Your findings may help influence data-driven decision making, so consider what communication methods may work best for your audience.

Work Geographic Pockets of Wealth

If generating increased numbers of major gifts is your goal, make time to conceptualize what can be done to target the wealthy in geographically concentrated areas.

Examples might include:

- Selecting specific ZIP codes in your community or service area and conducting particular direct mail efforts.
- Regularly visiting and networking in locations throughout the nation that have higher concentrations of wealthy constituents.
- Coordinating get-acquainted receptions of any sort in wealthy neighborhoods throughout your community or region.
- Convincing an existing board member or donor to purchase a gift membership for your CEO to exclusive clubs where he/she can rub shoulders with persons of means.

Use Predictive Modeling to Find Potential Donors

Prospect research and donor stewardship are about specific individuals — those who could donate or those who already have. Predictive modeling, in contrast, concerns generalized profiles, not individual people. By identifying attributes that correlate with an increased likelihood of giving, a predictive model creates a picture of a typical supporter, allowing an organization to make educated guesses about who will give and who will not.

Peter Wylie, a recognized expert in the field and author of "Data Mining for Fundraisers," answers questions about this area of fundraising that can be as misunderstood as it is promising:

In simple terms, what is predictive modeling in a fundraising context?

"Predictive modeling is basically a way of using data to build an algorithm, a score, that generates a profile of people who might not have given a lot of money yet, but look and act like the people who have. It's a way to know which lower-level givers your gift officers should be paying more attention to."

Can you give an example of what this would look like in practice?

"Say you're a university and you pull a Microsoft Excel file of 20,000 alumni records. You start by assigning attribute fields: 1) unique identification number, 2) total lifetime cash given, 3) a home phone appears in the database — yes or no, 4) business phone — yes or no, 5) e-mail — yes or no, 6) marital status, 7) preferred year of graduation, 8) ever attended any event after graduation — yes or no.

"Once you have that, you look for relationships between any field and the outcome variable, the amount of donation. Married donors will probably give more than single donors, for example, and widowed donors will give even more. So you assign a numerical score for each attribute, apply the formula to everybody in the database, and categorize people based on composite score. Some of the top scorers will already be under stewardship, but others you will have never heard of, and those are the people you want to introduce yourself to."

Is there a minimum number of donor records needed to generate meaningful results?

"Most small nonprofits either don't have something that could be considered a true donor database, and therefore, can't do predictive modeling, or they have thousands of files, which is plenty to make reliable decisions."

How do behavioral attributes like having attended a reunion compare in importance to demographic attributes like age or ZIP code?

"The more behaviors like opening an e-mail, attending an event or volunteering you can count, the better. Demographic information can be behavioral, but it doesn't have to be. Someone might have given you their business phone, but a gift officer might have just looked it up. Someone might have given you their mailing address, but you might have acquired it somewhere."

Are there data points nonprofits should be tracking but often aren't?

"Electronic data is one of the biggest areas. At any event where people are using membership cards — a museum, a symphony, a ticketed fundraiser — there is data that can be stored — so much that you can learn quite quickly what kinds of events people go to, what subject areas they prefer and so on. All this can then be correlated to donations.

"The other big area is web metrics — tracking the relationship between online behaviors (like) opening certain kinds of e-mails, visiting certain parts of a website — and giving habits. This is a promising field, but its challenge is that website software often gives aggregated data instead of personalized."

What steps might an organization take in exploring predictive modeling?

"A good first step is just seeing if you can pull information out of your database and put it into spreadsheet format. You can do some pretty good initial analysis without even needing a statistical software package. Reading the CoolData blog would also be helpful."

Source: Peter Wylie, Author, Data Mining for Fundraisers, Washington, D.C. E-mail: pbradwylie@aol.com

Comprehensive Wealth Sweep Jump-starts Major Giving

When Patricia Laverty became director of philanthropic giving at Rocky Mountain PBS (Denver, CO) in early 2010, she discovered the major gifts program barely scratched the surface in cultivating true major gifts. To kick-start the program, she used a comprehensive wealth sweep to mine major and planned-gift prospects from its 55,000-member database.

"We have a very large donor base because of our on-air fundraising and direct mail programs," says Laverty, "but finding major donors in this haystack is difficult."

She used the research firm Target Analytics®, a Blackbaud Company (Charleston, SC), to focus her efforts by analyzing her database. "Target Analytics uses publicly available financial data. The overlays that we purchased gave me likelihood ranges for both planned giving and major gifts," she says. "You can buy different products, and each one is a finer filter."

Rocky Mountain PBS used liquidity, hard assets, community connections and philanthropic donations screens to shake out 12,500 promising names from its database, with even more detailed liquidity information on 5,000 of those, and hard asset profiles on a further 500 names.

"Before we did the wealth screen," Laverty says, "I used our Cornerstone Society, which is a group of about 350 people who give to our local PBS network at a higher annual level, as my base to cultivate, but it was too small, and I found that some of these people were unable to become major donors."

The membership database used by many PBS stations includes interest codes for members that Laverty uses in developing personal relationships with prospects. "People want to give to something they're passionate about. When our producers come to me with a local program idea, I'm beginning to know who might be interested in sponsoring it."

Similarly, a $10,000 investment in wealth sweep is paying back exponentially for Clemson University (Clemson,

SC), says Bobby Couch, executive director of major gifts.

"Our wealth sweep generated well in excess of $2 million in new money," Couch says. "And we've only begun to scratch the surface."

The sweep began when development staff submitted 55,000 names from a donor database and athletic ticket database to prospect research firm Wealth Engine (Bethesda, MD). Couch says they then sliced and diced the resulting reams of data to create a workable list of 3,500 persons capable of $100,000-plus gifts. The list included both prospects who appeared in university databases but were unknown to development staff, and long-term supporters of the program who had not been approached for a major gift.

The results were eye-opening, he says. "People we'd never have guessed turned out to have the capacity to give at significant levels of support, and some we didn't know at all."

They divided the 3,500 names into geographic markets and financial capacity. Given the volume of names, staff had their hands full just approaching the $1 million-plus category. Couch estimates that only around 10 percent of the 3,500 have been contacted.

Couch says conducting wealth sweeps every three to five years is ideal. He also recommends a frank assessment of internal resources before undertaking such a venture. "If you do not have the staff to support the results, the data will just sit on a shelf and you will not get a return of your investment," he says, noting that his development staff has doubled since its first sweep five years ago, and is still expanding to meet the work demand generated by the sweep.

Sources: Bobby Couch, Executive Director of Major Gifts, Clemson University Athletics/IPTAY, Clemson, SC.
E-mail: Jcouch@clemson.edu
Patricia Laverty, Director of Philanthropic Giving, Rocky Mountain PBS, Denver, CO. E-mail: patricialaverty@rmpbs.org

Develop a Predictive Model to Identify Likely Givers

Knowing your prospects can help you develop successful fundraising strategies.

Staff with the Arkansas Children's Hospital Foundation (Little Rock, AR), turned to the DonorCast analytical system to better understand and solicit donors. DonorCast, by Bentz Whaley Flessner (Minneapolis, MN), is a people-driven analytics system that helps nonprofits understand their people, enhance their programs and realize their potential.

"We didn't have enough prospects identified to meet our fundraising goals for an upcoming comprehensive campaign," says Enid Rorex, the foundation's lead research analyst. DonorCast helped them create a predictive model highlighting persons in their database likely to be annual, major and planned gift donors.

"DonorCast is not wealth screening, which adds external asset data to individual records," says Rachel Hurlbert, DonorCast operations's associate director. Rather, DonorCast integrates that capacity knowledge with an organization's internal data indicators of a prospect's level of connection, interests and giving history to create a comprehensive propensity, or likelihood, rating.

The program helps identify and prioritize prospects, forecast fundraising potential and tailor fundraising activity and staffing, Hurlbert says. It helps build in-house analytics programs by providing consulting, training and collaborative modeling.

The foundation uses DonorCast primarily to segment and prioritize constituents for annual gift appeals and prospect for major gift and planned gift donors.

"By using DonorCast to prospect from those who are likely to be major gift donors to our institution, we've decreased the suspect-to-prospect ratio," Rorex says. "Of names being researched, approximately one in three are passed along to a gift officer. This has increased the efficiency of the prospect research department and has resulted in gift officers spending their time focused on prospects with both capacity and inclination."

Sources: Rachel Hurlbert, Associate Director of DonorCast Operations, DonorCast, Minneapolis, MN. E-mail: rhurlbert@bwf. com. Enid Rorex, Lead Research Analyst, Arkansas Children's Hospital Foundation, Little Rock, AR. E-mail: rorexec@archildrens.org

Available Database Screening Methods

The four basic types of database screening methods are:

1. *Demographic* —

   A rating is assigned to each prospect based on demographic factors such as ZIP codes and age. This method is generally imprecise and may lump together groups at census block level, thereby incorrectly rating those with post office boxes or in mixed areas.

2. *Modeling* —

   Different patterns are used to rate prospects with this method, from past giving and demographics to what magazine subscriptions they hold. This can be helpful if done internally, based on profiles of what an organization's best prospects look like. Some vendors provide ratings using proprietary modeling software, so determine what criteria they use for their ratings to be sure this method fits your needs.

3. *Hard Assets* —

   Specific pieces of data, such as real estate ownership, stock holdings and business affiliations, are tied to individual prospects with this method. This allows for assigned ratings due to wealth indicators and follow-up analysis based on giftable assets.

4. *Dynamic* —

   The next generation of screening, this method takes hard asset and demographic data to the next level by including analytical reporting software as part of the product that is returned to the organization. Users can then apply their own modeling or add other data from their own research to after a more complete picture and more precise rating of a prospect.

Steps to Choosing, Reusing a Vendor

Whether it's your first contract or your fourth, if you are considering working with an outside vendor to provide screening information, you'll want to make sure to complete the following:

Preparation — Determine your goals and priorities, set a timeline for need and implementation, and examine your budget and support structure.

Shopping — Review lists of companies, get references, attend product demonstrations, ask for free trials, submit a request for proposal (RFP) and narrow your choices.

RFP components — Ask for technology requirements, establish what data is sent/received, get minimums and pricing, find out about client support and training, and include updates and maintenance schedules/pricing in the contract.

Taking delivery of data — Integrate the information into your database or a separate system, determine who has access to the data, assign staff for training and establish what staff time is required.

Reviewing data — Run reports on selected groups to check the accuracy of the data and its ease of use.

Processing data — Confirm results for all prospects, identify prospect groups, run standard and ad-hoc reports, and tweak the data as needed.

Analysis — Track the use of the results, determine your return on investment, analyze the support you receive from the company and accuracy of the data and decide if additional screening is necessary (on the same group or additional prospects).

Get the Best Use Of Screening Results

The information provided by screenings will only help you if they are well-utilized. Otherwise, they just become expensive bits of data. To make the best use of your efforts, follow these tips:

- Fill in gift tables with names once results are analyzed.
- Focus on the top-rated prospects who are givers over the last three to four years. Set up a cultivation plan and timeline for that group.
- Assign top rated prospects — new and past donors — to appropriate staff for solicitation strategies.
- Invite the top rated new prospects to group events such as galas, dinners, auctions and golf tournaments, to introduce them to your mission and begin relationships.
- Invite the top-rated new prospects to participate in advisory groups as a way to increase their knowledge of and commitment to your organization.
- Segment rated prospects for special mailings — planned giving, higher annual giving or special topic newsletters.
- Find connections between prospects to help build relationships with the organization and to identify potential solicitors.

Determine the Frequency of Screening and Rating

Most research activities should anticipate frontline efforts by one to two years, so screening and rating projects need to be done prior to any campaign kickoff.

Once your campaign gift table is established, you'll have a better idea of the type and number of prospects you'll need to identify for your campaign. As you move through your campaign, you'll also be able to tell if you need to conduct additional prospecting to fill holes in your gift table, based on ranges of giving.

Screening and rating projects depend a great deal on the size of an organization's database and the staff available to oversee them. Larger databases tend to need to have more frequent screening efforts to identify the better prospects, but organizations also need the staff — both in number and ability — to tackle the screenings, analyze the results and

determine the ratings.

The frequency of redoing projects also depends on the types of screenings you undertake. Vendor database screenings that provide hard asset information should probably be refreshed at least every few years. Peer screenings are more subjective, and generally don't need to be redone as often. You might consider annual contracts that allow for new data on any prospects you've added to your database or to update subsets of your priority prospects.

Review any ratings you have established every two to three years to determine if you need to update any of them, especially if there have been any significant changes in economic or asset aspects for your prospect pool. Periodic review also makes sense if you have added a number of new prospects to your pool since the last rating took place.

Peer Screening Overview

When conducting peer screening sessions, methods you have to choose from include:

- **One-on-one**, which involves a staff member meeting with a volunteer to go over a list of prospects;
- **Silent review**, accomplished with a group writing information on lists; and
- **Group discussion**, where the group talks about the prospects and a staff member writes down the comments.

You can categorize your prospect lists and review groups by geography, profession, class/age or social circles, and include vendor-identified or rated prospects.

Benefits of this process include getting new and updated information, the ability to categorize and prioritize prospects, receiving subjective and anecdotal data you may not find elsewhere, plus the fact that the process is relatively simple to implement.

Friend-raising benefits of peer screening sessions include connecting with constituents who serve as reviewers, helping volunteers connect with each other, developing a volunteer network, creating opportunities for marketing your organization and building excitement among a select group.

Drawbacks may include additional staff time, meeting-associated costs, a timeline that doesn't allow for scheduling sessions, subjective results that may vary greatly from volunteer to volunteer, and the need for follow-ups with the data and volunteers.

Peer Screening Process and Timeline

Before you launch into a peer screening, make sure you understand the process and set up a detailed timeline to follow. Here are some tips:

1. Determine groups to review.
2. Establish a plan.
3. Set the session format(s) and decide on location(s).
4. Recruit volunteers and hosts.
5. Schedule the sessions.
6. Mail invitations to volunteers.
7. Make calls to confirm attendance.
8. Prepare formatted lists of prospects.
9. Set up systems to record data and track results.
10. Conduct the sessions.
11. Send thank-you notes to volunteers and hosts.
12. Compile results and analyze the data.
13. Prepare analytical reports for staff.
14. Follow up on reports by incorporating prospects in moves management strategies.
15. Inform volunteers of successful results.

Four Keys to an Effective Peer Screening

A well-run peer screening — the right people given the right names and the right kinds of instruction — can be a highly effective tool for major prospect research.

Unfortunately peer screening often falls short, says Scott Tomlinson, campaign director at Arena Stage, a Washington, D.C.-based theater.

If you are considering a peer screening, Tomlinson says it is imperative to do the preparation needed to give those participating a meaningful sense of contribution. In particular, he says to make sure that you have the right:

- **Names.** "If you are giving your group a list of 1,000 or 2,000 names, make sure they will know at least some of them. If your group members are graduates of 1980, give them a list of 1978 to 1982 prospects, and give them an overlay of ZIP codes as well, for added context."
- **Process.** An effective screening needs to be efficient, and that starts with precise workflow guidelines, says Tomlinson. "Tell participants that you are going to give them a 500-page list with four names on every page, and that if they don't know the person within the first 10 seconds, they don't know that person well enough to give them a rating, and move on."

- **Questions.** The success of a screening also depends on the criteria used to rate prospects. "The central question I have participants consider is: 'How much do you think this person could give over the next five years?'" says Tomlinson. He also stresses the importance of getting and recording as many anecdotal details about prospects as possible.
- **Focus.** A productive peer screening is looking for people of capacity, but primarily people who represent new or untapped potential, says Tomlinson. "Every city has a couple dozen people that everybody knows, everybody wants money from, and everybody knows lots of information about. Those individuals can be put on the list, but don't spend much time on them. Look for new resources."

Tomlinson says peer screenings can be a great way to engage board members, other key supporters and insiders in the development process. He also says that peer screening can be especially effective when carried out using the results of a third-party, electronic wealth screening.

Source: Scott Tomlinson, Campaign Director, Arena Stage, Washington, D.C. E-mail: Stomlinson@arenastage.org

Preparation Leads to Winning Peer Screening Meetings

Is your organization looking for quality major gift prospects? If so, one of the best ways to find them is peer screening meetings, says Jennifer Liu-Cooper, senior director of development and alumni relations services at the University of Delaware (Newark, DE).

"Two really clear benefits come from peer screening meetings," says Liu-Cooper. "First, you're cultivating the screeners themselves. They are often flattered to know you consider them a good source of information, and involving them deepens their connection with your organization. Second, you can not only locate potential prospects, but also identify peers who might be willing to solicit them."

An effective screening starts with thorough planning. Liu-Cooper recommends a major donor or board member host the screening, regardless of whether or not it is held at the individual's home. She says the host should be well-prepared with details of exactly what they are expected to do, and should be briefed on everyone who will be attending the screening.

In putting together an invitation list, Liu-Cooper says an attendance rate of about 20 percent should be expected. Building a group of 10 to 15 screeners, therefore, requires extending about 50 invitations. She advises requesting an RSVP from invitees and dating it two or three days before the screening. This gives development staff sufficient time to prepare individualized screening lists.

Screening lists are heavily influenced by the invitation list, and vice versa, says Liu-Cooper. "Putting together a list of people that each screener will know is of primary importance." To do so, she suggests screeners be given prospects from their own geographic area, industry area, decade of graduation or similar grouping.

The composition of the prospect lists or "books" can vary according to circumstances, says Liu-Cooper. She has used books with only 25 profiles, one person to each page. She has also used books with 200 names that are based primarily on check-boxes and use one overall section for notes at the end.

The most important thing, she says, is including plenty of questions that ask, "Would you be willing to contact or solicit this prospect?". She also advises listening to the informal conversation between screeners, as an additional source of information.

For organizations undertaking a first-time screening, Liu-Coopers says managing expectations is critical. "If you're asking people to help you, you really need to manage the expectations of what the results will be. If you don't follow through in the ways you've told them you will, it will be difficult to approach them again in the future." This entails follow-up phone calls to the screeners, thanking them for their participation and discussing next steps regarding the prospects.

She also says one-on-one screenings can be useful. "They can be the only way to accommodate some people's schedules. Also, more high-powered people sometimes don't want to be part of something done en-masse. So you should never hold off on a one-on-one just because you're planning a group screening in the future."

Source: Jennifer Liu-Cooper, Senior Director of Development and Alumni Relations Services, University of Delaware, Newark, DE. E-mail: jliucoop@udel.edu

Well-conceived support materials, such as this, can greatly enhance the impact and efficacy of a peer screening.

Content not available in this edition

Peer Screening 101: Anatomy of a Session

Heard people talking about peer screening sessions, but not quite sure what one would look like in practice? Jennifer Liu-Cooper, senior director of development and alumni relations services at the University of Delaware (Newark, DE) is here to help.

"A peer screening can be done in a variety of ways," she says. "If your organization doesn't have a lot of means, you can start with a meeting of board members, a board of trustees, an alumni association board, or a similar group — people who already have a toe in your support efforts and are a captive audience."

The session should involve no more than 15 people and should last between an hour and an hour and a half, says Liu-Cooper. "You want 15 to 20 minutes for a speaker to get them pumped up. Next you should have 10 to 15 minutes explaining the premise behind screening and how to do it. Then 30 to 40 minutes to go through the books, depending on the size of your list."

Liu-Cooper says the questions presented to screeners should focus on basic issues of linkage, ability and interest. "The most valuable piece of information is what they think the prospect's capacity is. But you also want to know whether or not they are in good financial health, whether they are philanthropic and whether they are active in the community."

Liu-Cooper also offers a few more helpful tips.

- Instruct screeners to comment only on people they actually know.
- Urge screeners to add names that aren't on the list, but they think should be.
- Make sure screeners know that any comments they make will be held in confidence. This will allow them to share their thoughts more freely.
- Make sure prospective screeners (e.g., those who have been invited but have not yet accepted) know they will not be solicited at the session.
- Don't invite people you are currently soliciting to act as screeners.

Tips to Maximize Your Prospect Screening Sessions

Are you planning prospect rating and screening sessions among board members, donors and friends of your organization? Maximize the results by incorporating these tips:

- Develop a planning time line by beginning with the screening session date and working backward.

- Segment who screens various prospect groups: Those in the same profession as the screener; those with similar philanthropic interests as the screener; those who reside in the same geographic area as those being screened.

- Limit the sessions to two hours or less to respect participants' time, then be sure to start and stop on time.

- Hold sessions at locations that are the most easily accessible for the majority of attendees and perhaps hold some drawing-card appeal (e.g. the exclusive home of a board member).

Three Great Times to Use Prospect Screening in Campaigns

When is the best time for prospect screening in a capital campaign? Organizational circumstances are the final arbiter, but Lawrence Henze, managing director at Target Analytics, a Blackbaud company, says three major phases — before, during and after a campaign — can be productive options, each for different reasons:

- **Before the campaign begins**. Prospect research can be accomplished as late as the quiet phase of a campaign, but ideally should be done sometime in the year before, says Henze. "Campaign goals can be self-fulfilling prophesies, so it's good to know how much capacity is in your database when doing feasibility studies and goal setting." Increased knowledge of your fundraising potential may give you the confidence to pursue loftier goals.

   A pre-screening can be used to verify the assets of previously identified top-level prospects, but Henze says the most effective result is often identifying untapped mid-level potential. "Widening the middle section of your donor pyramid has two benefits," he says. "First, it can result in significant donations in the short term. But more importantly, it identifies top donors for future campaigns."

   Henze says another advantage of pre-campaign screening is that it can identify tremendous planned giving potential. "Planned giving is often overlooked in capital campaigns, because it doesn't address the need for current dollars. But planned giving can and should be part of a major capital campaign."

- **In the middle of the campaign**. Henze says mid-campaign screenings are usually prompted by one of two situations. The first is when an organization has seen such success in the first half of a campaign that organizers are considering raising the goal. "This can be particularly effective from a predictive modeling standpoint because the data generated by the campaign allows a model to be much more robust and accurate going forward," he says.

   The second situation Henze refers to as the "sweaty palms" scenario: when organizers are worried they won't make their goal and are looking to back-fill their donor pyramid. He says that while donors can be identified in this way — he notes that most organizations in this situation failed to undertake a screening in the first place — if prospects are not giving already, the typical cultivation time of at least two to three years is often too long for a campaign's time frame.

- **After the campaign ends.** Post-campaign screening focuses as much on the next campaign as the last, says Henze. Like mid-campaign screening, recently gathered giving data (including planned giving prospects) can be used to more precisely identify prospects for future solicitation. But screening can also help refine performance and identify organizational strengths and weaknesses, says Henze. "You hit your goal of $100 million, but is it possible you could have hit $150 million? You made your participation goals, but will you be able to count on your primary donors for the majority of your next campaign? These are the kinds of questions a predictive modeling screening can help answer."

Source: Lawrence Henze, Managing Director, Target Analytics, a Blackbaud company, Charleston, SC.
E-mail: Lawrence.henze@blackbaud.com

Wealth Matters Less Than You Think

 What is the biggest misconception people have about prospect screening?

"That knowing who is wealthy is still the most important piece of information. Major gift officers really want to know how much people are worth before initiating a conversation, but all the research I've done over the last 18 years suggests that someone's affinity to give is much more important than their capacity to give. For one thing, people are coming up with more and more creative ways to hide their assets. But more than that, by putting so much emphasis on visible wealth, we ignore the giving potential of people who can give six- or seven-figure gifts through planned giving. For many organizations, the dollar potential of planned giving is much greater than cash giving, and many times these prospects are not identified through wealth analysis"

— *Lawrence Henze, Managing Director,*
Target Analytics (Charleston, SC)

Rating, Screening Procedures

- There are two basic types of screening: a) one in which the group moderator goes down a list of names and those present share what they know about each prospect while staff take notes and b) a list of prospects is distributed and participants silently make notes about anyone they know, then turn them in at the end of the session. The first method works best for smaller groups (10 or fewer) while the second is more appropriate for larger groups.

Understand Your Prospect

People will always look at the cost-to-benefit ratio once they've decided how much to contribute. Knowing that fact in advance — as well as other unique characteristics of each donor — will help you anticipate where to best focus your efforts.

What Screenings Can Uncover

Database and peer screenings can help make the difference in whether or not your campaigns and major gifts programs are successful. While some screening methods will turn up subjective data, the utilization of the results can drive programs for many years. Let them point you to the cream of the crop among your prospects and donors by uncovering items such as the following:

Capability — General wealth factors to help determine giving ability.

Readiness — When to ask for the gift.

Interest and Propensity to Give — The prospect's belief in your mission.

Project Target — Program or area that would most interest your prospect.

Giftable Assets — Multiple properties, stock holdings, art collections, etc.

Connections to Others — People, corporations, foundations; for solicitation of that prospect or to establish the prospect as a solicitor for another.

Business Information — For tracking career, connections to other people or wealth factors.

Philanthropic Giving and Inclination — Giving to your organization and others to gauge potential gift amounts.

Prospect Research Fundamentals: Proven Methods to Help Charities Realize More Major Gifts, Fourth Edition.
Edited by Elizabeth Dollhopf-Brown.
© 2012 Stevenson, Inc. Published 2012 by Stevenson, Inc.

CONNECTING WITH POTENTIAL DONORS AND MANAGING PROSPECT INFORMATION

To build and sustain your program, you must be able to track and maintain information on the prospects and donors you identify, cultivate, solicit and steward. This "system" allows you to manage hundreds of major gift prospects and donors simultaneously, paying attention to each detail of action directed to and received from everyone in your system.

Track Prospects Through Development Cycle

Most seasoned fundraisers know the development cycle well: Identify potential supporters, qualify/verify their financial capacity and interest, cultivate their relationship with the organization, solicit their support and steward their continued involvement.

So vital is this progression of relationship to effective fundraising that every prospect management system should identify which stage — identification, qualification, cultivation, solicitation or stewardship — prospects are in at any time and note how long a prospect has been in that stage.

This information allows organizations to answer questions critical to the fundraising process, such as: What percentage of prospects are currently at what stage? How has this distribution of donors changed over time? What is the average length of time to advance a prospect from one category to the next? How does the progression of major donors compare with that of smaller annual donors? Where are prospects getting hung up in the cycle?

Ask the Right Questions in Major Gift Discovery Calls

Discovery calls are key to keeping a donor pipeline stocked and healthy, says Eli Jordfald, senior major gifts director at UNC Lineberger Comprehensive Cancer Center (Chapel Hill, NC).

"A discovery call is a call to a prospective donor — someone who may or may not have given in the past — with the aim of finding out if cultivation toward a major gift is appropriate," Jordfald says. "The goal of the call is not necessarily to get a visit, but to determine if a visit is warranted.

"Past donors who have consistently given at lower levels are a great constituency for discovery calls," she says. "Other groups include first-time donors who have given several hundred dollars, individuals who have given generously to causes similar to yours, and individuals who have been suggested by board members or other major donors."

Jordfald advises fundraisers to approach discovery calls as an opportunity to listen, not talk. She also suggests structuring the conversation around three sets of questions:

1. **Questions that assess interest in the organization, including:**

- "Tell me about your experiences with our organization."

- "Would you be interested in learning more about our research and programs?"

- "How do you see your involvement with the work of our organization?"

2. **Questions assessing financial capacity, including:**

- "Where do you work and in what capacity?"

- "Do you have plans to travel?"

- "Do you have favorite organizations you like to support? Tell me about your involvement there."

3. **Questions that determine next steps, including:**

- "Would it be convenient for me to visit you in a week or two?"

- "I'd like to invite you on a tour of our facilities. Would you like to schedule a time to do that?"

For organizations embarking on a discovery call program, Jordfald recommends incorporating calls into a weekly schedule. Above all, she says, just enjoy the conversations. "It's really a lot of fun to talk with people who are interested in your organization. When you ask the right questions, you'll be amazed how many wonderful and informative conversations you will have. It's a great use of time."

Source: Eli Jordfald, Senior Major Gifts Director, UNC Lineberger Comprehensive Cancer Center, Chapel Hill, NC.
E-mail: eli_jordfald@med.unc.edu

If You Want a Mega Gift, Create a Mega Plan

Here are some strategies to help you focus more time on identifying and cultivating mega gifts:

❑ **Enlist a major gifts committee.** Assemble a committee that is willing to help develop ways to approach prospects capable of contributing $1 million or more.

❑ **Conduct research.** Once you have begun to identify mega prospects, research them. What you learn may provide the thread that eventually connects them to your institution.

❑ **Enlist key centers of influence.** Identify those centers of influence who are already committed to your organization and can play key roles in influencing your prospects.

❑ **Identify the prospect's agents of wealth** — Those professionals who serve your prospect (e.g., estate planning attorneys, financial planners, accountants, trust officers, etc.) — to determine the roles they might play, if any, in supporting your effort to approach and solicit the prospect.

❑ **Design a plan for each mega prospect.** Based on what you have learned about each prospect, develop a plan of introduction and cultivation leading toward the eventual solicitation of a mega gift for your organization.

Develop long-term plans to identify, research, cultivate and solicit mega gifts.

PROSPECT CULTIVATION PLAN

Name _____

Residence #1 _____
City _____ State _____ ZIP _____
Phone (_____) _____

Residence #2 _____
City _____ State _____ ZIP _____
Phone (_____) _____

Occupation _____

Business Address _____
City _____ State _____ ZIP _____
Phone (_____) _____

IDENTIFIED CENTERS OF INFLUENCE
1. _____ 4. _____
2. _____ 5. _____
3. _____ 6. _____

IDENTIFIED AGENTS OF WEALTH
Attorney _____ Broker _____
Accountant _____ Other _____
Financial Planner _____ Other _____

KEY CULTIVATION STRATEGIES	ANTICIPATED TIMING	KEY PLAYER(S)
_____	_____	_____
_____	_____	_____
_____	_____	_____
_____	_____	_____
_____	_____	_____
_____	_____	_____
_____	_____	_____

Essential Profile Information

Don't Let Prospects Fall Through the Cracks

The prospect management report is a tool that helps fundraisers stay focused on prospects needing continued cultivation or solicitation. It helps visualize the process of bringing each prospect closer to the realization of a major gift over a specified time period. The report is particularly helpful when managing a large group of prospects for a project or program.

The report can be updated each month and should provide an ongoing record of activities that have taken place with each prospect and a clear picture of what needs to occur with each prospect over the next 30 days.

Although you will no doubt want to design a prospect management report that best fits your own organization, you can use the model illustrated here as a way to get started.

Here are some tips for using this report:

Solicitor: List the individual responsible for eventually soliciting the gift. It may be a staff member or volunteer.

Manager: This is the person responsible for managing the ongoing identification, research, cultivation, solicitation and stewardship of the prospect pool. The prospect manager may or may not be the solicitor.

Prospect: Simply refers to the name of the prospect.

Prospect's region: You may or may not have use for this criteria, depending on the geographic size of your prospect pool. You may wish to substitute another criteria such as gift type or prospect constituency.

Likelihood of gift: This criteria represents a judgment call on the odds of getting a gift. P = poor, F = fair, G = good, and E = excellent. Forcing a decision on the likelihood of a gift every 30 days helps prioritize the amount of attention a prospect should be receiving.

Gift size: Refers to the size of gift you are seeking from the prospect.

Movement: Refers to the amount of activity that has taken place with the prospect in the past 30 days. [0] refers to no activity, [-] refers to negative activity and [+] refers to positive activity. For instance, if you have had no contact or communication with the prospect, you would list [0] in that category. If, on the other hand, the prospect had become irritated by something your organization did, you would list [-] for negative movement in the past 30 days.

Personal time: How much measurable time/effort have you (or someone associated with your nonprofit) devoted to the cultivation or solicitation of this prospect in the last 30 days? Simply list the amount of time in terms of hours or portion of an hour.

Months needed for decision: How many months will it be before you get an answer on whether or not the prospect will contribute to your program? In some cases, it may take less than one month. In other instances, it may take as long as 24 months.

Personal time: Refers to the amount of time you plan to devote to the prospect during the next 30 days.

Type of next contact: Will you be phoning the prospect, drafting a proposal directed to the prospect, or meeting face-to-face with the prospect? Once again, the criteria helps to prioritize the way in which you plan to bring the prospect closer to the realization of a gift.

Comments: This category provides an opportunity to list special circumstances specific to that prospect. They may pertain to the past 30 days or the next 30 days.

Content not available in this edition

Learn From Prospects' Philanthropic Histories

When calling on a new prospect for the first time, don't underestimate the abundance of what you can learn based on questions about his/her past gifts to other charities. The answers you receive may provide clues regarding the best solicitation approach to take in the future, insight into the individual's funding interests and more.

Here are some sample questions you can use to gain insight into a prospect's past giving to other causes:

1. "I know you have been a very generous contributor to a number of causes in our city. As you look back, which one or two gifts brought you the greatest satisfaction? Why?"

2. "I'm always interested in learning more about people's philanthropic philosophy. Do you have any principles you follow in deciding how to apportion yearly gifts? Do you give on a first-come, first-served basis, for instance, or try to plan your philanthropic budget for the year?

3. "You mentioned that you have given regularly to (name of nonprofit). What do you suppose it is that compels you to give to that organization so generously?"

Maximize Prospect Management With Focused Contact Reports

Contact reports are the heart and soul of prospect management. Without accurate, reliable and quantifiable reports, management systems, no matter how sophisticated or comprehensive, will be haphazard and limited.

However, in many organizations, the sophistication of the management system is not matched by efficient and productive procedures for using it. In short, the potential of the system is not effectively tapped.

The following policies, developed by officials at Georgia State University (Atlanta, GA) and codified in the Georgia State University Prospect Management Procedure, give one example of how a uniform standard of reporting might be achieved:

Contacts and contact reports:

Substantive contact. A substantive contact is an intentional and meaningful interaction with a prospect that is significant in advancing the prospect in the prospect management cycle.

Examples of substantive contacts:
- Personal visits in which discussion of the prospect's affinity to the university, desire to make a gift or other pertinent information is shared.
- Significant telephone conversations in which the status of a prospect's affinity or gift is discussed or clarified.
- Significant e-mail contact that moves the prospect closer to making a gift to the university.

Examples of non-substantive contacts:
- Routine correspondence such as thank-you notes, greeting cards, etc.
- Chance meetings at place of worship, the mall, the supermarket, parties, etc.
- Casual conversation at an event or board meeting.

Contact report content. A contact report must be entered whenever a development staff member has a substantive contact with a prospect that moves him or her closer to a gift.

Contact reports should:
- Be written in the third person.
- Take care in reporting sensitive and confidential information which may become public through media and legal inquiries.
- Include participants, purpose, results and follow-up.
- Employ an inverted pyramid style which places significant information in the first or second sentence and arranges other details in order of decreasing importance.
- Record next actions, dates and assignees at the time the contact report is entered.
- Report objects of affinity (philanthropic interests and will-not-give-to), degree of affinity ... and inclination.

Source: Georgia State University Foundation, Atlanta, GA. E-mail: foundation@gsu.edu

Minimize Staff Resistance To Prospect Management

To be effective, prospect management systems require commitment, dedication and more than a little data entry. For this reason development officers often feel it means extra work for development and fundraising staff.

To minimize potential staff resistance to additional duties, gift officers need to be shown how they will benefit from a proposed system, not just be told to support it.

In particular, they need to be given accurate and timely data that advances projects that are meaningful to them.

Encouraging frontline officers to take ownership in system outcomes will go a long way in smoothing the transition to a more systematic and results-based fundraising program.

Utilize Contact Reports to Stay Organized for Prospect Analysis

Every development officer knows how important it is to keep track of personal and professional details about their donors. The more information you have on hand when meeting with a donor, more robust your prospect analysis will be.

Contact reports contain a lot of vital information: how well the donor is informed about a campaign, personal details about the donor's life, giving his- tory, gift potential, major mile- stones in your relationship with the donor (such as the ask and the gift), donor's preferred timeline, even the emotional state of the donor in response to various elements of your conversation.

By keeping contact records of your donor meetings, your organization can maximize your capacity for donor information.

This system allows you to stay organized: to keep track of what was discussed and when, personal details and events in the donor's life, where the organization and the donor stand in terms of progress on a gift, how and when to plan the next meeting with the donor.

Streamlining donor meetings in this way may even promote radical thinking — perhaps you notice a pattern in your donor meetings that would have otherwise gone unnoticed and can offer insight into strategy Maybe you make connections with disparate donors, and realize that the approach with one donor might apply to your blossoming relationship with another. Maybe two donors could become partners in leadership on a project.

Keeping records of these important meetings creates a permanent record of your relationship with a prospect, for current analysis and future reference.

CONTACT RECORD

Constituent name: Mrs. Jane Doe

Contact Information (if unchanged from database): Already in contact database

Contact Type: ☑ Personal Visit ☐ Telephone Visit

Date of contact: 9/9/2011 **Contacted by:** Development Officer Smith

Prospect Interest: Pediatric Oncology

Purpose of the contact: It was Mrs. Doe's 65th birthday (Sept. 9)

Brief summary (notes): I took Mrs. Doe to her favorite restaurant, Italiano's, where we began by discussing her family: Husband Al Doe, son James Doe, daughter-in-law Jenny Doe and their son (her grandson) Jimmy Doe Jr., nickname "JD." JD is suffering from pediatric leukemia and has been for 5 months. Mrs. Doe again brought up the prospect of donating to the fund for Pediatric Oncological Research, and said she would like to meet again next month to discuss further, after JD has finished his next round of treatment. I did not make an ask at this time, but we made tentative plans to meet again in October.

Changes: Mrs. Doe now prefers to be reached on her cell phone, 612-555-1234.

Any additional comments: Mrs. Doe is very sensitive to term "cancer" in regard to JD. She refers to "the leukemia," or "his condition," and seems to prefer others follow suit.

Outcomes of Contact (please complete one section below):

☑ **This is a Major Gift prospect with whom I have already been working**

Next Step & Date: Contact again next week to schedule meeting to make ask. Prepare preliminary/informal giving plan proposal.

☐ **This is a New Major Gift prospect for my unit** (we will assign you as solicitor)

1. Prospect Status: ☐ Cultivation ☐ Proposal Development ☐ Negotiation/Closing

2. Gift Potential:

☐ $100,000,000 or more	☐ $50,000,000-99,999,999	☐ $25,000,000-49,999,999
☑ $10,000,000-24,999,999	☐ $5,000,000-$9,999,999	☐ $2,500,000-$4,999,999
☐ $1,000,000-2,499,999	☐ 500,000-$999,999	☐ $250,000-$499,999
☐ $100,000-249,999	☐ Requires Research on Estimated Giving Capacity	

3. Prospect Strategy: _____

4. Next Step & Date: _____

☐ **This is a Major Gift prospect who should be handled by another member of the organization.**

　　*What unit/MGO do you recommend?

☐ **This is not a Major Gift prospect at this time** *(Please provide 1-2 sentences explaining this outcome)*

_____
_____

☐ **Stewardship Visit**

Prospect Strategy: Very little needs to be done to push Mrs. Doe at this time. She is in a sensitive place regarding her grandson's care, and seems ready to give, if given the appropriate space and information.

Next Step & Date: Schedule meeting (ask), Sept 16, for the week of Oct 2.

Do you need a proposal added or updated? ☐ Add ☐ Update

Date Asked/Funded: _____

Amount Asked/Funded: _____

Gift Type: ☐ Deferred ☐ Outright ☐ Pledge

Instrument: _____

Track Cultivation of Major Donor Prospects

The prospect management report is a tool which is helpful in planning and monitoring the systematic cultivation of major gift prospects. Although estimates vary among consultants, assume a single fundraiser can manage the cultivation of 100 prospects if he/she spends 80 percent of his/her time in major gift cultivation. (If he/she spends less time in major gift cultivation the number of prospects able to be managed throughout a year would decrease).

If each prospect should receive an average of eight cultivation moves each year (toward the realization of a major gift commitment), it becomes important to have a manageable way of monitoring those cultivation moves, whether they are simple as a birthday card or as time-consuming as a joint fishing trip.

Maintaining a portfolio of reports on assigned prospects and donors can help in following a planned cultivation schedule and ensure that each prospect is receiving the attention that is required to realize a major gift.

Whether it's a phone call, written correspondence or an interview for an article in your magazine or newsletter, date all contacts you have with major prospects (under the appropriate category) to ensure that prospects are being appropriately managed. Each contact should, in one way or another, strengthen your nonprofit's relationship with that prospect.

Also, be sure to list events or programs that will serve in cultivating all prospects throughout the year (under the "Scheduled Cultivation" category).

Use the Comments section to highlight information that may affect future cultivation calls.

The individual prospect management form will help you stay focused on those who can give the most.

HILLCREST FAMILY SERVICES

Prospect Management Report

Prospect _____ Title _____
Spouse _____ Business _____
Address _____ Business Address _____
City/State/ZIP _____ City/State/ZIP _____
(H) Phone _____ (W) Phone _____
(H) E-mail _____ (W) E-mail _____

	LETTER	PHONE	E-MAIL	PERSONAL VISIT	SCHEDULED CULTIVATION	COMMENTS
JANUARY						
FEBRUARY						
MARCH						
APRIL						
MAY						
JUNE						
JULY						
AUGUST						
SEPTEMBER						
OCTOBER						
NOVEMBER						
DECEMBER						

CONNECTING WITH POTENTIAL DONORS AND MANAGING PROSPECT INFORMATION

Ways to Find Your Lost Constituents

Keeping track of your constituents is probably one of the most important tasks of any fundraising organization. If you don't know where they are, you can't keep them informed about your programs, you can't thank them for their gifts, and you can't solicit them for additional funds. Here are some suggestions for tracking constituents and what you can do to try to find them once they are lost.

- **Set up a computer database with the capability of marking records for mailing purposes.** Be sure to send mail to active records while excluding inactive ones. Also, you will need some sort of reporting mechanism to target lost records for tracing purposes.
- **Include "address correction requested" on your mailings.** This costs you extra, but if you mail third class, it may be the only way you will know if your mail is being sent to the right address. (Third class mail is not forwarded as a general rule; it may be thrown away if the address is incorrect.) Even if you use National Change of Address (NCOA) vendors regularly, it is a good idea to send at least one mailing each year to your entire constituency with the "address correction requested" statement. Check with your local U.S. Postal Service representative for recommendations and a current list of NCOA vendors.
- **Send regular surveys to your constituents.** These can provide helpful information in addition to mailing addresses. Ask for business addresses and phone numbers, fax numbers, e-mail addresses and any other items which might prove useful to your organization. The more ways you have to contact constituents, the easier it will be to track down someone who is lost. College and university surveys often ask for a list of degrees from other institutions and relatives who also attended their alma mater as a means of building ties and finding contacts to trace lost alumni.
- **Produce a constituency directory.** Directory publishers will often produce surveys for you as part of their service and some offer constituent tracing at no charge. Their costs are covered by the price your constituents pay for the directories. If you have a membership for which a directory would hold some appeal, check into this solution. Know what the publisher is offering you up front,

however, and check with other groups which have used their services.

continued on page 41

Resources for Finding Lost Constituents

AlumniFinder: An online tool to find lost alumni and other constituents. Most areas are updated daily.

Boyd's Alumni Research Services: A service of Boyd's City Dispatch, it helps find lost constituents, in addition to correcting and appending mailing information for ZIP codes and street names, new area codes and phone numbers. They can also indicate deceased records, provide Social Security numbers and flag potential donors.

DirectoryNETmail: In addition to providing more than 180 million current directory assistance listings, they also provide access to more than 80 million opt-in e-mail addresses.

Harris Connect: It helps you locate lost alumni, past members and other constituents using a variety of powerful search tools and databases. Services and products include directories, data cleaning services, NCOA, e-mail/phone number append, customized segmentation tools and predictive modeling.

KnowX.com: This site provides access to a number of public record databases. Some searches are free, but there is always a fee to view results.

Polk City Directories: An up-to-date online directory of every U.S. city. Search locally or nationally to find a person, business or nearby neighbors.

Telematch: Computerized U.S. and Canadian telephone number appending for phone numbers, it has more than 12 million residential phone numbers and more than 14 million business phone numbers.

Yahoo! People Search: Yahoo! provides a free search database for mail and e-mail addresses and telephone numbers.

CONNECTING WITH POTENTIAL DONORS AND MANAGING PROSPECT INFORMATION

continued from page 40

- **Use tracer cards to get updated information.** Send them to relatives and employers if you have lost your constituent member, or mail them to constituents to verify new addresses when you learn of them. In addition to making sure a home address is correct, ask for a new phone number, business address and phone, and any other pertinent information. The cards are also appropriate to send to constituents who are newly married or have new jobs for updated names and addresses. Some organizations send this type of card as a combination update form and letter of congratulations.

- **Online databases can provide a wealth of information.** In addition to Directory Assistance products which give you addresses and phone numbers, some services will even give you selected demographic data, including income and housing information for the constituent's area. You are charged per record searched, but some of them will only charge you if you find information. The Internet also has a number of sites which contain this data for free.

- **Many avenues are available to you if you are able to send groups of computer records.** Some tracing services include NCOA vendors, companies which provide telephone numbers, and organizations which can give you data based on last known address and/ or Social Security number. You will generally pay less per record to use these services than you would for address-correction-requested postal returns or an online database search; discounts are often available for larger record groups. It is a good idea to utilize this service on a quarterly basis to catch people closer to the dates they move. Costs are often negotiable, so contact your area representative to see if you qualify for any discounts.

- **A key factor in determining whether batch tape updates work for your organization depends on your ability to process the information once you get it back.** A review process, utilizing either report printouts or an online program, is key to the success of any of these services. You may have better information than the vendors in some cases, for a variety of reasons, and should check their data before you load it over yours. Most NCOA services can provide you with an effective change date which can help you determine whether or not their information is more current than yours. Check with other organizations that have used these services before you sign a contract. This will help you judge how you will need to prepare for the process.

Name_____ Student#_____
Degree & Year_____
Maiden Name_____
Address (On File)_____
E-mail_____ Phone#_____

If Above is Correct, Check Here ☐
If Incorrect, Please indicate corrections below:

Name_____ Degree_____
Home Address_____
_____ Phone #_____
Business Name & Address_____
E-mail_____ Phone #_____
Married?_____ Spouse Name_____
Spouse Alumnus/na?_____
Name Under Which Attended _____
Degree & Dates Attended_____

Tracer cards are used to verify new addresses and seek additional information. The self-mailer has a message and address printed on one side with the verification information and organization's return address printed on the other, making it simple to complete and return.

The University Alumni Office is continuously updating the records of more than 200,000 graduates and former students. This information is only for official use of the University.

We would appreciate your personal confirmation of the information on the reverse side of this card. Please indicate if our information is correct. If not, please make the necessary changes.

Additional data will be useful for your personal biographical file.

PLEASE
RETURN
TODAY!

Manage Prospect and Donor Information Effectively

The success of any fundraising program is based on the ability of its staff and volunteers to handle information. This includes tracking data on prospects and donors, as well as setting up systems to make more efficient use of time. It's important to know what to collect, how to keep it and how to use it effectively. Advances in technology and the increasing availability of useful information should help you become more efficient. By addressing who, what, when, where and how, your information management system should fit the needs of your program.

Who collects the data?

Researchers. If you have a separate research office, these staff members can be a vital element in collecting background information on donors. They are also helpful in turning up new prospects, and can suggest fundraising strategies based on their findings.

Volunteers. Committees, board members and friends of your organization can play an important role in your program. In addition to acting as contacts and conduits for gifts by individuals and organizations, they can provide you with lists of new prospects, help you rate prospects capabilities and giving interests, and give you inside information.

Development personnel. Frontline staff can be instrumental in discovering information from direct contact with the prospects and donors, in addition to performing background research on their own. If possible, it is best to have fundraisers spend most of their time in the field, and let other staff and volunteers collect and manage the data.

What do you collect?

Biographical data. The basics, such as name, address and phone number, are critical to your success. Make sure you have some method to collect and maintain this data so it is as accurate as possible. Nothing irritates a donor more than having his name misspelled on a receipt or in an honor roll listing.

In addition to the basics, try to find business information, family and other personal connections, education data, awards, hobbies and interests. Aside from being good topics of discussion, they can help you identify keys to possible giving capabilities and focus areas.

Affiliations. It is important to know the connections donors and prospects have to your organization and to other organizations. This will help you determine their commitment to your cause and their giving interests. You may also be able to discover ties they have to other donors and prospects.

Sample Donor Profile

CONFIDENTIAL	
Name:	ROBERT LEE BAKER "BOB"

Occupation/ Title:	Baker Energy Corporation
	    Chairman and Chief Executive Officer
	Baker Oil and Gas Company, Inc.
	    Director
	Transnational Pipeline Company, Inc.
	    Chairman of the Board

Business:	Baker Energy Corporation 1500 Smith Street, P.O. Box 1100 Shreveport, LA 71109-1100 (318) 754-6774
Home:	3195 Inwood Drive Benton, LA 71006-3225 (318) 655-1008

Education:	AB Economics 1962
	MA Economics 1963
	LLD (Honorary) 1985
	PhD Economics 1972
	    University of Texas at Austin
	Borah High School 1958
	    Boise, Idaho

Spouse:	Second: <u>Linda Sue Davis Baker</u>
	    Non alumna
	    (Degree and dates unknown)
	    Married: July 10, 1985
	First: <u>Jennifer Diane Miles Baker</u>
	    BJ News Editorial 1965
	    Married: June 10, 1965
	    DIVORCED (Date Unknown)

OU Participation:	OU Alumni Association, Life Member B&PA Citation of Merit, 1988 B&PA Executive-In-Residence, 1988 College of Engineering Awards Banquet Speaker 1975 Phi Beta Kappa Omicron Delta Kappa Dean's Honor Roll

Continued on page 43

CONNECTING WITH POTENTIAL DONORS AND MANAGING PROSPECT INFORMATION

Continued from page 42

Financial information. Although it is often difficult to find this type of data on private companies and individuals, you can collect indicators of wealth. Compensation and stock holdings can be found on public company insiders, and real estate information is available on just about everyone. You can also find data on the ownership of planes, boats, luxury cars, etc. Many resources have financial data on companies and foundations.

Philanthropic data. It is essential to have accurate and detailed giving information on your donors. This not only gives you an idea of their capabilities and interests, it helps you officially recognize them and move them to the next level. Collecting data on giving to other organizations is also useful.

When do you collect information?

Assessment. During the assessment phase, you should be gathering information on new prospects and donors. As you identify prospects, you should rate their capabilities and inclinations to give to your organization.

Cultivation. Once you discover that prospects and donors are capable and willing to contribute, they enter the cultivation (or friendship-building) phase. During this stage, you will collect background information and track all of your contacts with them.

Solicitation. When the prospects are ready to make a significant gift to your organization, you should track the solicitation data. Prior to the ask you will need to know what areas of interest they have and how their gift can fit into your program. Corporations and foundations have specific funding priorities and proposal guidelines, and you should be aware of these before you prepare your solicitation. If possible, you should have a system to track solicitations before and after they are completed as an aid in setting and meeting fundraising goals. This will also help guide you in future solicitations of the same donors.

Stewardship. After solicitations have been successfully completed, donors move into the stewardship phase. You should continue to track contacts with them during this period, as well as significant events as they occur. You will also want to monitor their financial "well-being" and other philanthropic activities. This phase goes hand in

hand with continued cultivation and should be used to prepare donors for their next gifts.

Continued on page 44

Sample Donor Profile

Page 2

OU Scholarships:	President's Scholarship
	National Association of Manufacturers
	Monroe Fellowship
	Exceptional Student Fellowship, Prudential Co.
Civic and Philanthropic Affiliations:	Louisiana State University
	Chairman of the Board of Regents
	Louisiana State University Board of Visitors, Chairman
	Shreveport Metropolitan YMCA, Director
	LSU Foundation, Director
	Shreveport Chamber of Commerce, Member
	Shreveport University Club, Board of Governors
	U.S. Chamber of Commerce
	National Resources Committee, Member
	John Lloyd Museum, Atlanta, GA, Director (1974-1976)
	Marietta (GA) Library, Director (1974-1976)
Business and Professional Affiliations:	President's Energy Council, Member
	Energy Advisory Board, Committee Member
	Clean Air Act Advisory Committee, Member
	Interstate Natural Gas Association of America, Member
	National Petroleum Council, Member (Former Board of Directors)
	American Economics Association, Member
	Baker Hughes, Inc., Director
	Microsoft Computer Corporation, Director
	Transnational Pipeline Company, Director
	First City National Bank of Shreveport, Director
	Louisiana Bancshares, Director (1990)
	Baker International Corporation, Director (1990)
	National Economics Club, Former Member
Other Giving Interests:	Louisiana State University
	In 1989 Baker had given $1,000 annually for several years. He was solicited for a capital campaign leadership gift in 1989.
Birth Date:	April 15, 1940
	Caldwell, Idaho

CONNECTING WITH POTENTIAL DONORS AND MANAGING PROSPECT INFORMATION

Continued from page 43

Where do you find the information?

Internal records. This is the first place to look for data on your prospects and donors, and it should include correspondence, clippings, survey forms, past proposals and any computer database information you have stored.

Periodicals. There are numerous regional and national newspapers and magazines on a variety of topics which can be of value. Look for articles which provide clues to your prospects' philanthropic capabilities and interests. Business periodicals and press releases can also inform you of promotions, job changes, company mergers and staff changes at organizations.

Publications. A number of books exist which provide varying levels of information on individuals, corporations and foundations. They range in scope from regional to international, and some of them focus on specific subjects such as lawyers, private companies and targeted funding sources.

Online information. You can access a number of online databases and some of them are free. Periodicals, stock transaction data, real estate holdings and many business publications are available online. In addition to certain newspapers and corporate annual reports, you can access selected stock and financial data on public companies. You can also use online resources to communicate with individuals, companies and foundations, and electronic discussion lists provide excellent networking opportunities.

Libraries. Regional public branches, university and college centers, and other specialized libraries often have many of the sources listed above. In addition, a number of professional organizations have reference centers which will provide information to their members.

Public records offices. Property assessments, divorce and will settlements, and lawsuits are generally public records. These records can provide you with concrete financial data on your prospects and donors. You may need to visit the court or office where the data is filed, but much of the data is accessible online, and some offices will give you the information over the phone.

How do you handle the information?

Hardcopy files. If you don't have the equipment to scan information into a computer, you will need to keep items such as correspondence, newspaper clippings, proposals and annual reports in an accessible filing system. You may segregate the files based on their ratings as prospects or donors, or separate the files on individuals from the corporations and foundations. However you set it up, make sure you have a procedure in place for maintaining the files, including a checkout policy for the central files. A key to a good filing system is to avoid duplication, including copies of data which you may be able to access elsewhere.

Computer databases. The most important tool you can have to manage your information is a computer. Whether you use PCs or networks, utilizing computers can make your operation more effective and efficient. Use them for recording addresses and phone numbers for mailings and other contacts, as well as tracking pledges, gifts and solicitations. Computers can help you manage your program by tracking the contacts you have with your prospects and donors, and you can set up ticklers to plan your next steps. If you have a large staff or a number of volunteers, a database system can serve as a traffic light as you assign prospects to specific individuals. This helps you avoid multiple concurrent and uncoordinated solicitations of corporations, foundations and wealthy individuals.

Retrieval. Files need to be accessible and available, and reports need to be meaningful and easily produced. Don't store information that you will not be able to retrieve or won't need. The best report in the world is useless if it doesn't serve your information needs or you can't get it when you need it. For this reason, defining your reporting needs is just as important as defining your database storage needs. In addition to being able to pull lists of prospects based on a variety of criteria, you will probably want to set up tracking histories of contacts with your prospects and donors, next step reports and a basic profile format for individuals, corporations and foundations.

Elements to Include in Your Prospect Management Meetings

Prospect management meetings can range from exhilarating and indispensable to stultifying and redundant. What should your meetings include? One Chicago, IL-based fundraising consultant suggests the following:

- Prospect assignment and/or reassignment
- Strategy development on an individual or collective level
- Review of individual or group activities and unstopping

progress when necessary

- Review of aggregate progress — pools or groups of prospects such as all Boston-based prospects or all $25,000 - $50,000 prospects
- Full portfolio audits when necessary
- Review, assessment and formulation of policies and procedures

Refine Techniques for Approaching Heirs of Inherited Wealth

Heirs of inherited wealth have a different relationship with their money than do people whose wealth comes from revenue earned in their lifetimes. The manner in which development officers approach these heirs should differ in kind.

Tom Wilson — 25-year fundraising consultant, and vice president and western regional manager, Campbell & Company (Portland, OR branch), which provides consulting services to nonprofits in areas of advancement planning, fundraising, marketing communications and executive search — has identified key points to remember when dealing with inherited wealth.

Wilson says identifying heirs is different than identifying other potential major donors. Younger people are much less likely to become philanthropic, but may begin engaging in behaviors early on that identify them as potential donors down the line.

"One young man I dealt with began purchasing real estate in his early 20s to get his feet wet," Wilson recalls. Another young woman began making numerous $10,000 donations around her community because she felt she was too young to make a larger gift of higher profile. "To me," Wilson says, "that said she was trying to get noticed."

It is worth a fundraiser's time to establish relationships with younger heirs apparent early on. "Get them to adopt you," he says.

Overall, listening is the most important tool when dealing with heirs, because of the sensitivity surrounding the finite nature of their wealth. "Don't assume (heirs) are going to be generous," he says, "They've got to protect this asset. Knowing how to protect money is different from knowing how to make money."

Wilson says it is important, therefore, for development officers to listen actively to the attitudes that heirs have toward their money. Listen for the answers to the following questions, even asking them aloud when appropriate:

❑ What is the heir's role when it comes to the inheritance? Does he/she want to guard it, share it or grow it?

> ### Understanding Age Factor in Major Giving
>
> Tom Wilson has been fundraising for 30 years, raising hundreds of millions of dollars for hundreds of clients.
>
> Wilson, vice president and western regional manager, Campbell & Company (Portland, OR branch), and author of "Winning Gifts: Make Your Donors Feel Like Winners," says a client recently asked him to count how many $1 million-plus donations came from donors under 40 years of age.
>
> His reply? "Two. And they were both inherited wealth."
>
> Wilson's theory for this pattern: Younger people are less likely to give because they don't know if they will maintain their income and often have yet to worry about major expenditures like tuition or home ownership. Young entrepreneurs are less likely to give because they are often too busy with their businesses.
>
> Still, establishing relationships with potential donors early in their careers is prudent, he says: "You may be talking about a 20-year relationship, but you never know when someone will turn philanthropic."

❑ Is the heir the first person in the family to potentially guide family philanthropy, or does a legacy of giving already exist? Is a family foundation in place? Who are the trustees?

❑ What are the heir's interests? Where do his/her passions lie? How are heir's intentions for wealth similar to or different from the person from whom he/she inherited it?

Once you as the development officer have answered these questions, you can navigate the relationship in a way that best marries your needs and the desires/passions of the heir. Above all, dealing with heirs takes patience. There are many complex feelings involved when a person is in a position of inheritance. As Wilson says: "It's important to realize it's going to take time to heal, and that attitudes will change over time. It's a moving target. But if there's a high gift potential, it's worth it."

Tom Wilson, Vice President, Campbell & Company, Portland, OR. E-mail: tom.wilson@campbellcompany.com

Prospect Research Fundamentals: Proven Methods to Help Charities Realize More Major Gifts, Fourth Edition.
Edited by Elizabeth Dollhopf-Brown.
© 2012 Stevenson, Inc. Published 2012 by Stevenson, Inc.

Financial ability is the key ingredient for determining if an individual or business should be included in your prospect pool. Once a prospect passes your minimum requirements for financial ability, it becomes a matter of prospect prioritization. Following are several methods and tips for assessing donors' giving potential.

Methods for Assessing a Donor's Giving Potential

The ability to determine a person's net worth for the purposes of fundraising is a myth that has been perpetuated for years. Even if you know the majority of a person's assets, you most likely will not know all of his or her liabilities. And you have to know both to know the net worth.

That doesn't mean you can't estimate an individual's raw capability to donate. There are a number of formulas and guides available for this purpose, and trial and error may be needed to figure out the best one for your constituents.

Following is a sampling of some of the more popular assessment methods, including some hypothetical examples, illustrated at left. Just remember, you still have to convince the person to give to your cause.

In seeking to assess a donor's giving potential, keep in mind:

1. Liquidity is key, unless you are looking for donations of property. Even stock holdings may not be available for donations in certain circumstances.
2. Annual gifts are generally based on income and capital gifts are based on assets.
3. Consider age, number and ages of children, lifestyle, and cost of living for the location.
4. Only stock holdings for insiders and owners of 5 percent and above are reported and available as public information.
5. Assets held in trusts are difficult to find through research.
6. Information on executives and directors of public companies is much more readily available. Proxy statements can be very helpful in identifying income, stock holdings, company loans, retirement plans and other indications of wealth.
7. Those in real estate and agriculture are often land-rich and cash-poor.
8. Owners of private companies may be putting all of their earnings back into the company. On the other hand, they may be getting additional perks from this affiliation, such as home allowances, cars, paid vacations, etc., that would offset usual living expenses and leave them with more liquidity.
9. The ownership of valuable property can be expensive to maintain. This includes lavish homes, ranches, art collections, cars, boats, etc. Consider property taxes, insurance, hired staff, and other costs as liabilities when figuring assets and worth. Remember that assessed value may have no relationship to purchase price or market value.
10. Stock brokers and investors usually have a higher proportion of their wealth in stocks and bonds. Venture capitalists generally have more cash, but it may be tied up in investments.
11. Income estimates are available for many professions in several sources.
12. Ratings and net worth estimates are available from several electronic screening vendors. Ask how they arrive at their figures before using the data.

Content not available in this edition

Four Rules of Thumb for Estimating Major Prospects' Assets

Prospect research provides many kinds of information, but few carry as much weight as a prospect's total net worth. All other information is judged in relation to this gold standard.

Unfortunately, net worth is information that no prospect research system will fully uncover, says David Lamb, senior consultant at Target Analytics, a Blackbaud company (Charleston, SC).

However, he says it is something that can be estimated, and he offers the following estimation methods:

- 5 to 10 percent of annual income
- (Total real estate) x (4) x (5 percent, when real estate value is greater than $500,000)
- (Total stock holdings) x (4) x (5 percent, when stock value is greater than $100,000)
- 5 percent of all known assets, when assets are greater than $1 million

These simple rules of thumb are based on national averages and will produce only rough estimates of net worth. Nevertheless, Lamb says the figures they generate provide a suitable starting point for conversations with major donors. "You know you'll at least be in the right ballpark, and you can go from there," he says.

Source: David Lamb, Senior Consultant, Target Analytics, a Blackbaud Company, Parker, CO. E-mail: david.lamb@blackbaud.com

Go Into Prospect Research With Realistic Expectations

Prospect research can reveal a great deal of information, but like anything else, it has its limitations. Having realistic expectations will help avoid frustration and make the research process more efficient and productive.

David Lamb, senior consultant at Target Analytics, offers the following thoughts on what prospect research can and can't do.

What you might be able to find:
- Where does your prospect live?
- Does she/he own property?
- Where does your prospect work?
- Does that employment contribute to gift capacity?
- Does the prospect give elsewhere? How much?
- Where is your prospect connected in the community?

What you will never know:
- Your prospect's net worth
- The size of his/her bank account
- Most investments
- Inheritances or family money

Research Source of Wealth When Measuring Giving Capacity

Giving capacity is arguably the most important factor in prospect identification. But closely linked to giving capacity is another important and often-overlooked aspect of donor research — the source of a donor's wealth.

Gleaning whether prospects have the funds they have promised, and that those funds are not ill-gotten, is a critical step in prospect identification.

The system of vetting potential donors is not elaborate; it is just an extension of the prospect research system which your organization should already have in place, says David Lamb, senior consultant, Target Analytics (Parker, CO). "When you think about giving capacity," Lamb says, "you are already thinking about the source of the wealth."

Poonam Prasad, founder and president, Prasad Consulting & Research (New York, NY) calls this process due diligence. "Your research and donor relation teams should already know about prospects before ever speaking with them," Prasad says, "what their interests are, their business history, financial history, giving history. This is the same thing."

But Prasad warns that excitement for a large donation can often trump due diligence. She cites a case of a major state university that announced a $1 million gift, which later proved to be an empty promise.

In other cases, Lamb says, "Organizations learn that a

donor obtained funds in a way that was antithetical to their values. It can cause a great deal of embarrassment."

In such cases, the problem lies largely in a communication disconnect. The research team may notice something amiss and not inform the donor relations team; the donor relations team may enter into a conversation with a potential donor without first asking the research team to vet them. For this reason, it is essential to keep all development team members aware of each other's actions.

Lamb suggests pre-empting the issue of gift source by writing gift policies: to decide ahead of time what kind of gifts the institution is willing to accept and which it is not. It is also important to make these policies well known throughout the organization.

In the same vein, be sure to share any discrepancies in a donor's history among departments. "If a donor has been giving at the $1,000 level and then suddenly gives $2 million, you may want to ask why," says Prasad. Donors should have transparent financial histories, with visible patterns. If something doesn't add up, speak up.

Sources: David Lamb, Senior Consultant, Target Analytics: A Blackbaud Company, Parker, CO. E-mail: david.lamb@blackbaud.com
Poonam Prasad, Founder and President, Prasad Consulting & Research, New York, NY. E-mail: poonam@prasadconsulting.com

Useful Research Sites

www.pretrieve.com — Search thousands of official public record sites to find free court records, free criminal records, property records and more.

www.domania.com — This real estate research site provides easy access to home values and real estate tools to help you with your property search.

Net Worth Formulas

One example of determining a prospect's net worth is to multiply his/her age by his/her total income — salary, dividend payments, etc. — and divide by 10.

Example: Annual income of $150,000 multiplied by individual's age of 54, divided by 10 equals $810,000.

Wealth Research Sites

www.publicrecordspro.com — Search for someone's anniversary, birth and death records and more. Cost: $2.95 per month.

www.vfinance.com — Scroll down to Site Shortcuts and click on Find Angel Investors to comb government records and gather investment data, industry preferences and stock positions of America's wealthy.

Electronic Toolkits Help to Identify Property

How important is the process of identifying property holdings in major prospect research? Hugely important, says Laura Solla, founder of Prospect Research & Development Strategies (Freeport, PA) and author of two books on the subject.

Solla shares some expertise on this critical aspect of the fundraising process.

Why is property so important to prospect research?

"Several reasons. Real estate is one of the few assets almost everybody owns. It is fairly easy to trace, even for a novice. And it gives a good indication of a prospect's overall potential."

Where should one start when conducting property research?

"If you have a particular address you're interested in, it's quite simple. Here are a few websites I recommend.

✓ "Zillow.com will give a valuation based on public record characteristics of a property. It is a great way to determine sellable value — what you could actually get for a property today — which is always preferable to assessed or market value.

✓ "Cyberhomes.com and ZipRealty.com are very similar to Zillow, and provide different source options to compare values. All of these services have plotted much of the U.S., but most databases will not show more rural areas."

And if you don't have an address?

"The data broker services Intelius.com and KnowX.com are great people-finder tools. For $2, you can enter a person's name and get primary address information along with age, phone number and other individuals living at the address. Keep in mind, however, that to effectively analyze overall wealth, the summer home in Maine or the vacation home in Florida is just as important as the primary residence."

What are some of the higher-end research tools?

"For organizations doing a lot of prospect research I recommend a subscription to Wealthengine.com, Donorsearch.net or Researchpoint from Blackbaud. Costing $1,500 to $3,000 a year, these subscriptions provide access to a real estate finder capable of identifying multiple addresses for the same prospect. They will also give access to databases indicating things like corporate affiliations, board affiliations and charitable giving."

With so many online services, is there any need to go to the assessor's office anymore?

"Rarely. Many counties now offer free online real-estate record searches. The only reason I see to actually drive down to city hall or the courthouse is if your geographic focus is local, you have several prospects to research, and your county does not offer an online record search. Aside from that, you can just do it from your office computer."

Contact: Laura Solla, Founder, Prospect Research & Development Strategies. Freeport, PA. E-mail: Solla@ResearchProspects.com

Financial Information Sources

You can never really know someone's net worth unless you know their total liabilities and assets. Even Forbes doesn't guarantee their wealthy lists to be 100 percent accurate. The best method for dealing with financial information as a gauge to someone's giving is to look at indications of wealth and liabilities as a general starting point rather than a final answer. There are a number of resources available to help you get a handle on some of this financial data.

- **10K Wizard** allows full text searches on SEC documents by company or individual, with highlighted section views, but requires a subscription to view full documents.

- Compensation data for the CEOs of some of the largest companies in the United States are included in the **AFL-CIO's Executive PayWatch database**. It also includes links to proxy statements for additional data.

- Sponsored by the U.S. Department of Labor, **CareerOneStop** provides information on wages and salaries by occupation and location, cost of living comparisons, and other useful salary and benefits data.

- **LendingTree's Domania** has a 30-million home database for historical home sales records (going back to 1987) and market values. In addition, you can determine estimated property tax.

- **EDGAR Online** gives you access to more than 15 million SEC filings, searchable by company name, ticker symbol, form type or keyword, and includes a free watchlist service with e-mail alerts, an IPO database and company profiles.

- **FindLaw's Firm Salaries and Other Statistics Charts** is a resource of base salaries and bonuses for law firm associations in select cities nationwide.

- **HEP Development Wealth Tracker** provides daily updates on job, stock, real estate and other activity of interest to prospect researchers.

- **J3 Donor Watch** provides tracking of donor and prospect stock portfolios and provides alerts to notify you of stock activity.

- **JobStar Central** provides links to more than 300 free general and profession-specific salary surveys. Some others are available for a fee.

- **Landings** allows free searches of airplane owners and certified pilots in its databases. Although not comprehensive like some pay services, it is a good starting point.

- **Market Watch** offers investing tools and data, including links to news, tracking portfolios you can set up, and insider trading reports searchable by ticker symbol or individual name. Big Charts (part of this network) offers historical quotes.

- **The Occupational Outlook Handbook** is a free site that includes descriptions and earnings for more than 250 occupations.

- **The University of Virginia's Research Department** provides links to assessors offices in the U.S. that have a presence on the Internet. It also has links to sites about aircraft, boats and horses.

- **Salary.com** provides information on compensation for a wide range of job titles. It is searchable by job category and ZIP or metro area.

- **The Salary Calculator** compares the cost of living in U.S. and international cities, and provides a link to U.S. tax tables to help you make additional salary comparison adjustments.

- **Christina Pulawski's Tax Assessor Database** has assessment to market value property ratios, links and office phone numbers.

- **Trulia** provides home prices, area trends and neighborhood research such as local schools, sales prices and real estate data.

- **Zillow** offers estimated values and more on 80 million-plus homes, and provides "heat maps" that reveal price ranges for homes in any area.

- Special issues are produced on an annual basis by **Forbes, Business Week, Fortune, Inc.**, and other magazines that list statistics for wealthy individuals, top level executives, etc. In addition, **business and industry journals** publish lists of salaries, profits, and board compensation for various regions and professions. They often list specifics for particular individuals and companies.

Public Records Provide Prospect Clues

Public court house records can provide a valuable source of information in researching major gift prospects. Utilizing public records can help you determine whether or not a prospect is worth pursuing for a major gift as well as an appropriate amount to request. Because the public records available at these offices contain information about people's private lives, researchers should examine their institution's code of ethics before pursuing this type of research. Also, a prospect may learn of your research since many public offices keep a log of who has accessed records.

❑ **The Assessor's Office** — The assessor's office often is of most value in conducting prospect research. You can generally determine the prospects's correct address, property values, spouse's name, and details that may provide clues to the individuals lifestyle, (having a pool, for example). If you know the county in which the prospect lives, you can look up the name of the prospect rather than the address, since it is likely he/

she might own more than one property. You will be able to determine whether properties are residential or commercial and learn more about the property itself. There will also be a breakdown of the property's assessments: land value, improvement value (the value of the building) and the total value.

❑ **Probate and Civil Court Offices** — The probate office can enable you to find information about an individual's inherited wealth. This is where you can review a will after it has been probated and the estate has been distributed. It can be helpful if a prospect has died and you wish to track who inherited their wealth, or if you know the names of those who may have willed assets to the prospect you're researching. The most useful source of information in the civil court office will generally be divorce records. These records, available only after the divorce decree is final, will detail an individual's assets and liabilities, including information about child support and financial settlements.

Sample Assessor's Office Information

Locator Number	Municipality	Land Use
Owner's Name		
	School District	
Property Location	Exterior/Interior Coml Information	
Property Description	Land Data	Building Data

7S-4-2-008-4 Ladue	110-Household Unit	Tax Dist - D
John Q. and Helen Donor H/W	R-Residential	Grnd Floor: 3399 sq. ft.
434 Steinway Place	121-Ladue	Style: Colonial
St. Louis, MO 63124	2000 - AC	Ext. Wall: Stone
	Topo -level	Heat Fuel: Gas
	Utility -all public	Heat System: Ht Water
Amended Lot 37 Plat BK-PG:	Access -paved	Attic: Finished
02-00787	-cul de sac	Garage: Masonry
		Pool: 25X050

Statistical Data	Sales Data	Values
	Price	Total - 1V
	Data Code	Land - LV
		Improvement - IV
		Total Taxes
# Stories - 2.0	Roll - Frame	$219,9401V
Year Built - 1929	7192-1262	$ 55,290LV
Total Rms -15		$164,650IV
Bedrooms - 7		$ 8,546 - 09/12
Bath - Full 6		
- Half 1		
Fixt-Addl 1		
Fireplaces:		
Woodstack 3		
WD-Opening 3		

Research Stock Ownership

A comparative study of estates by the IRS determined stock ownership usually makes up about one-third of a person's net worth. This, of course, is an average based on a number of individuals, and not an exact measure of any one person's wealth. It is, however, a good indication of the part which stock holdings can play in a person's financial picture. The amount of stock an individual owns can vary from day to day, but it is possible to find out about some stock which certain individuals possess.

Insiders

- By law, stock ownership is public record for individuals who are considered insiders of public companies.
- An insider is a person who is an officer or director of the company, or one who owns at least five percent of the company stock.
- Although a person is a company insider, you may be unable to get data on all of his/her stockholdings, since most investors have diversified portfolios.

Interpretation

- Although you may need a CPA to interpret some data, these SEC documents offer useful facts.
- The sections entitled "Summary Compensation Table and Stock Appreciation Rights and Stock Options Granted include a number of tables which list stockholdings for officers and directors.
- Read all of the footnotes, since much of the information will have further explanations.
- Check out the Retirement Benefits section for additional compensation information.

Stock Donations

- Stocks provide some indication of a person's overall wealth and can be donated to organizations fairly easily.
- A stock's value is generally determined by an average price of the shares on the date they are transferred to the organization.
- Although there may be capital gains inherent in the sale of the stock, an outright donation to a nonprofit organization can alleviate this tax issue for donors. This makes gifts of stock an appealing option for many philanthropists.

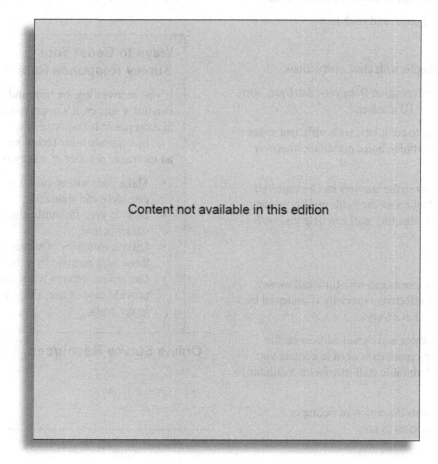

Content not available in this edition

Look Before Leaping Into Your Next Survey

Surveys can serve a variety of purposes. They can help you collect basic data as well as guide your organization as it serves your constituents. There are as many survey designs as there are organizations, from census forms for directories to attitudinal instruments, and no one layout can fill all needs. If you embark on a survey project, consider these aspects as part of the process.

Preparation

- Determine what you hope to discover with the instrument: better addresses, income data, donor interests, organization affiliations, etc.

- Stick to a few main goals and design your form around them. Keep it short, but make sure it fulfills your goals and information needs.

- Every question should have a clear purpose; ask only those for which the data will be useful to you.

- Get feedback from others in your organization on their data needs. Involve the data entry staff; they can make you aware of any coding standards you need to consider.

- Set a budget and timeline, and stick to it.

Design/Layout

- Keep the design simple, with clear instructions.

- Reprint any basic information from your database, such as name, address and ID number.

- Make the form easy to complete, with sufficient space for answers, and multiple-choice questions wherever feasible.

- Format the questions so the answers can be captured in your database. Make sure the fields and codes are coordinated. Your computing staff can help you with this.

Production

- Online survey instruments can save time and money, and are often more effective, especially if designed by someone well-versed in surveys.

- Include a phone number and e-mail address on the survey in case your constituents need to contact you. Make sure a knowledgeable staff member is available to answer questions.

- Give your constituents the option of faxing or e-mailing their responses to you.

- Offer a raffle prize to boost response rates and help gather contact information. Make sure you separate the contact information from the reports if the survey is supposed to be anonymous.

Follow-up

- Devise a method for following up with those constituents who did not respond. This can be a postcard, second copy of the survey, phone call, e-mail, etc.

- Once the processing has been completed, produce analysis reports for your organization. Make sure you use the data as you originally intended.

- Publish the results of the survey for your constituents, if applicable. This is one way to show them how the data was useful to your organization.

- Analyze the results to determine where the survey was successful and what mistakes you made in the design. This will help you plan your next instrument.

Ways to Boost Your Survey Response Rate

If you're investing the time and expense to conduct a survey, it's important to generate the highest possible response rate.

Incorporate these techniques to encourage an increased number of survey responses:

- Make your survey user friendly (easy to complete and submit).
- Include your facsimile number as a survey return option.
- Offer a summary of survey results free to those who respond by your deadline date.
- Use online surveys whenever possible to provide ease of use, simplified reporting and lower costs.

Online Survey Resources

- Constant Contact
- Survey Monkey
- Zoomerang

Complete Board Profiles Annually

If you don't already do so, ask both new and existing board members to complete a board member profile. Here's why:

❑ The background information can provide valuable data that may prove helpful in tailoring an eventual request that meets the interests/personality of that board member.

❑ The information can prove to be helpful in establishing rapport and cultivating your relationship with the board member.

❑ The profile will illustrate linkages the board member may have with other businesses and organizations — linkages that may prove helpful in opening the way for new or increased gifts.

Here is a list of information you may want to include in your board member profile form:

- Name
- Spouse's name
- Home address
- Second residence address
- Phone numbers and e-mails: residence(s) and business(es)

- Business
- Title
- Business address
- Primary nature of business
- Key linkages with other businesses/individuals (e.g., parent company, primary vendors, partners, etc.)
- Spouse's occupation
- Spouse's title
- Children (names, birthdates, locations, occupations)
- Civic organizations (past/present)
- Other boards (both nonprofit and for profit)
- Past recognition/awards
- Board member/spouse birthdays
- Anniversary

If you're able to secure this information when new members come on your board, it can be used in tailoring a standard news release announcing the board member's appointment to your organization, thus better justifying your request. As time passes, the completed profile information may prove valuable in numerous ways.

Searching for Professionals

Looking for background information on individuals in certain professions? These websites may help:

Attorneys:

- Martindale Hubbell has a free directory that can be searched by name, firm, corporate legal departments, government or faculty.
- FindLaw's Lawyer Directory allows searches for lawyers and firms by name, legal issue and location (including international searches).

Certified Public Accountants — CPAdirectory provides a centralized location for finding all CPAs in the U.S.

Dentists — WebDental's database can help you find a dentist by name and location.

Geologists — Geology.com includes a career section with articles about jobs, salaries and companies in the oil and gas, mineral, environmental and engineering sectors.

Physicians (Medical):

- DoctorFinder is a service of the American Medical Association and provides information on physicians in the U.S., searchable by name or specialty.
- LocateADoc.com has more than 160,000 doctors, dentists, surgeons and chiropractors in its database, searchable by specialty and location.

Musicians, Publishers and Writers — The American Society of Composers, Authors and Publishers (ASCAP) website has interviews, events and news. You will also find information in its Career Development section on the business and income sources for musicians, publishers, etc.

Real Estate Agents — The Real Estate Library offers a directory of U.S. real estate agents by state.

Securities Brokers — Financial Industry Regulatory Authority (FINRA), is the largest non-governmental regulator for all securities firms doing business in the United States. FINRA BrokerCheck is a free online tool to help investors check the professional background of current and former FINRA-registered securities firms and brokers.

Using Patient Databases in Healthcare Fundraising

In an age of increasing concern over an individual's privacy, hospital fundraisers might think twice about using patient records for donor information. Keeping in mind the confidentiality issues and HIPAA regulations, there are some pieces of data in those records which can be very useful for prospect and donor development.

If your hospital will provide access to the database, look for the following items:

Format. Work with the records department for direct database access, even if limited. Being able to check information online as needed is a plus. If you can't get online access, try to get selected information in reports. With reports you can manually check for specific data on prospects. You can also ask for reports on selected groups of individuals based on various criteria.

Contact Info. The database will have prospect addresses and phone numbers you may not be able to find elsewhere.

Birthdates. These are helpful in selecting planned giving prospects.

Relatives. You can sometimes build a track record of entire families who use your facilities, and this may make for a stronger case in your solicitation. It may even point to family-wide solicitations and named endowments.

Physicians. Linking prospects with their physicians can aid you in soliciting gifts from groups for special programs or physician honorariums. This can also help you identify potential areas of interest for specific prospects.

VIP Visits. Set up a system with your volunteer auxiliary or guest services department so you are both aware of VIP patients. Special touches, such as flowers or staff visits can help those patients feel important to your organization. Use caution, however, since not everyone enjoys being seen in a hospital setting.

Treatment Dates. If they feel good about the experience at your facility, patients and their relatives often contribute to hospitals with anniversary donations based on the date of their treatments. This can be true of births, heart surgeries, etc. Again, be careful how you use this data as some may not want to be reminded of their stays.

Useful Research Sites

- www.nozasearch.com — the world's largest searchable database of charitable gifts.

- http://boardreader.com — a fresh slant on researching prospects: enter any topic, including company name, to see online discussion and activity.

- http://world.maporama.com — Web and mobile mapping solutions that combine the strengths of geographical information and business intelligence.

- http://vlib.org — Run by volunteers, the WWW Virtual Library (VL) is the oldest catalogue of the Web, started by Tim Berners-Lee, the creator of HTML and of the Web itself, in 1991.

- www.grantsfire.org — an online service from The Foundation Center offering up-to-date information on grants.

Prospect Research Fundamentals: Proven Methods to Help Charities Realize More Major Gifts, Fourth Edition.
Edited by Elizabeth Dollhopf-Brown.
© 2012 Stevenson, Inc. Published 2012 by Stevenson, Inc.

RESEARCHING COMPANIES AND FOUNDATIONS

Corporations and foundations generally have very specific funding guidelines, and research plays a key part in the successful identification, prioritization and solicitation of these prospects.

How to Find the Best Corporate, Foundation Prospects

What is the best way to gauge the interest level of a foundation or corporation? Determine its capacity to give a major gift, affinity to your organization and interest in your programs, says Christina Pulawski, an independent consultant with Christina Pulawski Consulting (Chicago, IL).

"Does that corporation or foundation give its funds in the type of chunks that you need?" she says. "For example, if you need $100,000, and the foundation gives a maximum of $100,000, but in smaller amounts of $20,000, that foundation does not have the capacity to fund your project, or you will need to adjust your approach."

You can determine the prospect's affinity to your organization by looking at what ties the corporation or foundation has with your program. Do you have board members in common? Someone who can make an introduction? Are there other natural partners?

"The best organizational prospects are those with natural ties to your mission or goals, and that basically want the same outcomes your organization is trying to accomplish," she says. "They should also have an interest in your specific programs, and have strong ties to your community and constituency."

The goal of your initial research should be to produce a short list of prospects, says Pulawski. "At this stage, a print-out of what your organization does with a justification of why the funder is a good match should be enough to help decide whether to move forward or invest more time in building a relationship," she says. "You will also want to involve your organization's staff to find out who among them has ties to the corporate or foundation prospects on your list.

"Remember, building strong and long-term relationships with organizational funders is just as important as building donor relationships in individual fundraising — and should be planned accordingly," she says. "Sometimes the only difference is giving motivation or the approach method."

Your in-depth research will take place when you are actually preparing the proposal, she says: "That's when you make the most of your database, evaluate your connections to determine the best initial approach, look at your giving history, and research your off-the-shelf material (such as foundation directories), as well as conduct a thorough analysis of the foundation or corporation's prior relationship and giving history to see how it matches up with what your funding and timing needs are."

Source: Christina Pulawski, Principal, Christina Pulawski Consulting, Chicago, IL.
E-mail: c-pulawski@comcast.net

Be Proactive About Prospect Research

General prospect research should be an ongoing, proactive activity, says Christina Pulawski, an independent consultant with Christina Pulawski Consulting (Chicago, IL).

"The ability to be proactive comes from knowing your organization — its program and needs — and who your leadership connections are, and constantly mining them for whom they might know that might have a tie to a grant-making organization," she says.

Keep an eye on organizations similar to yours and who is funding them so that you can make sure they are in the queue for an approach from you, says Pulawski.

She shares other ways you can be proactive when conducting general prospect research:

- **Build on a known relationship.** You might have a lot of grantmakers who haven't funded you to the extent of their abilities. Take a close look at who is funding your organization and where you are on their hierarchy of giving. Are you at the top or the bottom? If you are at the bottom, why are you? Is it because you have not cultivated those interests as much? You want to make sure your funders are funding you at their capacity to give to you.

- **Focus your efforts.** If you know a project needs funding — or if you anticipate general funding needs in a particular area — identify a short list of funders whose interest and capacity might lead them to consider giving you a grant or initiating a cooperative relationship.

- **Prepare and present a proposal.** Once you have a known funder and project, make sure the proposal carefully follows specific guidelines and has the subtleties that will click all the triggers to be a success.

Look at Giving History When Researching Foundations

When researching foundations, it's important to look beyond their stated interests and restrictions to take a close look at giving history, which may reveal broader priorities, says Christina Pulawski, an independent consultant with Christina Pulawski Consulting (Chicago, IL).

Pulawski says that often, an organization's giving history is based on the interests of its board members or other leaders.

"As tacky as it sounds, I used to keep a liar's list of foundations that would fund outside of their stated interests, usually due to the interest of a board member," the independent consultant says.

This practice might indicate the presence of a discretionary fund for grants that can be used to fund a favorite organization or to allow a particular board member or family member to direct the funds, she says. Sometimes, she notes, foundations will provide funding to a location outside their designated geographic area because a board member happens to live at the location or for another such reason.

Once she identified a foundation that funded outside of its stated interests and restrictions, she says, "I would then focus on finding a way for our organization to connect with that foundation's leadership."

Source: Christina Pulawski, Principal, Christina Pulawski Consulting, Chicago, IL. E-mail: c-pulawski@comcast.net

Electronic Resources for Public Officer Research

Publicly traded companies are required to disclose significant information about top officers and directors. Where can this information be found? David Lamb, solutions consultant with Target Analytics (Parker, CO), suggests the following websites:

- "Yahoo Finance is what I usually use. It lets you search for a public company, pull up the company record and within the record there is a link that lists all the documents filed at the SEC."

- "Hoovers is a good site for corporate research in general. They compile quite a bit of information about public companies, along with an analysis of history and current status. They are fee-based, but offer some things for free."

- "J3 Services Group allows you to search for both company and insider information, and has a very user-friendly search interface."

- "10K Wizard from Morningstar Document Research is another fee-based service that is worth a look."

Source: David Lamb, Senior Consultant, Target Analytics, A Blackbaud Company, Parker, CO.
E-mail: david.lamb@blackbaud.com

To Determine Ask Amount, First Learn Value of a Prospect's Private Company Investments

With private companies being the greatest generators of wealth in the United States, prospect researchers would do well to learn of prospective donors' private company investments, says David Lamb, consultant, Target Analytics, a Blackbaud (Charleston, SC) company.

"Knowing the value of your prospects' private company investments can help you decide how large a gift they can make," says Lamb. "The problem is that word, private, which means they do not have to disclose information about themselves, if they don't want to. This makes it difficult to find accurate information."

Several resources can help you estimate a private company's value. Your prospect's title and history with the company and the percentage of the company that he or she owns can be important clues as to his or her capacity.

The best way to estimate the value of a private company is to find similar companies of known value. In that respect, valuing private companies is not unlike valuing real estate based on comparable sales, he says: "The more examples you can find, the better. Make sure the companies you find are a valid comparison. And be aware that a public company is almost always going to be valued higher than an equivalent private company."

Source: David Lamb, Senior Consultant, Target Analytics, A Blackbaud Company, Parker, CO. E-mail: david.lamb@blackbaud.com

Resources for Comparing Public to Private Company Value

David Lamb, consultant with Target Analytics, a Blackbaud (Charleston, SC) company, shares how to compare a prospect's private company to a similar public company:

1. Gather basic information about the company. Dun & Bradstreet can provide basic information such as sales, employee number, business type or Standard Industrial Classification (SIC) code.

2. Go to Yahoo Stock Screener and search by sales and industry categories using "find stocks."

3. Look for a public company the in same industry and region as the private one.

Don't expect to find an exact match. As public companies tend to be much larger than their private counterparts, you may have to use a sales range greater than the target's to find examples. Also, a public company with flat or negative earnings may still have value. Market capitalization (share price times outstanding shares) is one way to state a company's value.

Enterprise value is also a measure that accounts for company debt. You can then establish a ratio (or multiple) of annual sales to company value by a company's market capitalization or enterprise value by annual sales: Annual sales of $20 million and company value $10 million would give the company a multiple of 0.5. Find several companies in the same industry to establish a rough multiple to apply to other businesses in that industry.

Lamb offers additional resources to find data on public or private companies to compare to a prospect's private company:

✓ Consult specialized resources for business buyers and sellers, such as www.bizbuysell.com and www.bizstats.com/rulesofthumb.htm

✓ Business Valuation Resources works with business brokers to learn about private companies when they are sold. Pratt's Stats ($625/year) includes a database of 9,500-plus private company sales ($1 million to $14.4 billion) since 1990. Bizcomps ($425/year) has a database of 9,500-plus private company sales since 1993 — 61 percent with gross revenues under $500,000 and 18 percent at $1 million-plus.

✓ INC. Magazine's Ultimate Valuation Guide, an interactive chart, uses data from BVR (see above) showing how companies in various industries compare in median selling price, company value and median annual sales.

To estimate a private company's value, multiply estimate of the target company's annual sales by the value/sales multiple.

Using Your Research To Rate Your Prospect

After estimating your target company's value, follow these steps to rate your prospect, says David Lamb, consultant, Target Analytics, a Blackbaud (Charleston, SC) company:

1. Make your best guess at prospect's ownership percentage. Dun & Bradstreet may offer this. Lacking other guidance, divide ownership among named company officers of whom you are aware. If your prospect is one of four named officers, best guess is the prospect owns 25 percent. Consider other information you know about the prospect's relationship to the company. If it is named after your prospect, chances are prospect owns a larger percentage. Joe is probably the majority owner in Joe's Garage. If company is worth $10 million and you estimate 25 percent ownership, prospect's stake is $2.5 million.

2. According to the IRS, closely held stock is roughly 8 percent of a private company owner's net worth, but round it up to 10 percent to make it easy to calculate (and more conservative).

3. Multiply prospect's ownership (e.g., $2.5 million) by the IRS net-worth proportion (10 × $2.5M) to get your prospect's estimated net worth ($25 million).

4. Philanthropic capacity is often estimated as 2 to 5 percent of estimated net worth, so this prospect's estimated capacity is $500,000 (2 percent of $25 million) to $1.25 million (5 percent of $25 million).

As private company ownership is only one aspect of net worth, Lamb says, look at real estate and stock holdings to refine prospects' gift capacity estimates.

Uncovering Information on Private Companies

Locating company information requires tools and techniques that often differ from those used to conduct research on individuals. Private companies can be especially tricky to find since they do not have the same reporting requirements that public companies have to follow by law. There are millions of private U.S. companies, as compared to thousands of public companies that file information with the Securities and Exchange Commission. This is a good indication you will find a number of your prospects in the private sector.

Though the task of researching these organizations may be difficult, the following tips will make your search easier:

Start with basic sources (see below and Chapter 2). Resources that have details on a large amount of private companies include **Business Week's Company Insight Center, D&B's North American Million Dollar Database** and **Hoover's Online.** D&B also has its **Selectory®** business database that claims to offer company profiles for ALL private companies in the U.S. and Canada and 8 million firms from around the world. Databases such as **DIALOG** and **LexisNexis for Development Professionals** will also provide you access to various information.

Local companies can often be found in **area business directories** and other **regionally produced reference guides.** American City Business Journals annually produces regional **Books of Lists** which include data on various types of businesses. They are compiled from the Top 25 lists which are published in their business journals each week. Articles in **local business journals** can provide indepth information which is not found elsewhere. Even ads in newspapers and the Yellow Pages can be enlightening.

Several additional resources are available with information specific to international companies. **The Financial Times** has links to company news, backgrounds and financial data. **Forbes** has a variety of global lists that it produces annually. The **Search Engine Colossus** is an international directory of search engines with links to more than 350 countries. **ThomasGlobal** is the most complete, up-to-date directory of global industrial suppliers. You can search by product or company name.

There are also industry-specific resources. **ThomasNet** has basic information on North American manufacturers, and you can search by product, company name or brand name. **Business.com** contains listings in more than 65,000 industry, product and service categories. It includes hard-to-find categories such as agriculture, chemicals, pharmaceuticals, telecommunications and retail services. **Entrepreneur Magazine** includes its annual listing of top franchises, allowing searches by name, rankings or product/ service and lists business descriptions, financial data and contact information.

Reading national business journals and magazines, such as **Forbes, Fortune, Business Week,** and the **Wall Street Journal** can be invaluable in tracking private company information, and may turn up new prospects. Many of these publications are also available online. In addition, most companies have their own websites that include philanthropic information, which you can access for free.

The **chamber of commerce** in the company's area may have business information, and **area newspapers** often do stories on local organizations. **Honor Rolls** from other nonprofits often list gifts from private companies, and this can give you a good idea of their philanthropic interests and giving capacity.

All companies have to file certain information with the **secretary of state** for states in which they do business. The **state attorney general's office** may also have information on companies. If you know the company was involved in a civil lawsuit, you can access the **records from the courts.** These suits often require financial disclosures which have detailed data on various company aspects and that of its executives.

Check with **your network.** Your organization's employees and volunteers could have knowledge of the company through different means. Always double-check what you get from hearsay, though, as it could backfire on you. **Company visits** can provide a wealth of information in the form of brochures, annual reports, or knowledge of the location and workings of the business.

RESOURCES

American City Business Journals

Business.com

Business Week's Company Insight Center

D&B's North American Million Dollar Database

D&B's Selectory®

DIALOG

Entrepreneur Magazine

The Financial Times

Hoover's Online

LexisNexis for Development Professionals

Search Engine Colossus

ThomasGlobal

ThomasNet

Narrow Your Foundation Prospect List Early

Searching for possible funding sources can be an involved project. Although the process of defining your needs and narrowing your foundation prospect list to a manageable group can be a daunting task, it will save you time and effort in the long run. Up-front preparation will help you avoid sending out unnecessary (and possibly unappreciated) proposals. Keep these points in mind to help streamline the process:

Know your needs and define key elements. Many foundations have limitations in certain areas.

- What type of grant are you seeking? Do you need program support, capital campaign funding or endowment monies? Are you in need of equipment, building or renovation funds?
- Is the program mainly in the field of education, healthcare, religious or social service support?
- Does the program serve a local, regional or national constituency?

Know the guidelines of the foundations and their program areas.

- *Private* or *independent foundations* have broader giving ranges, but may have specific guidelines and limited programs. The proposals may be reviewed by the donor or members of the donor's family, an independent board or by a trust officer.
- *Company-sponsored foundations* are funded by corporations, but are set up as separate organizations. Grants are generally made to programs and organizations that relate to corporate activities and operating locations.
- *Community foundations* are set up with contributions from a number of donors in a region, and grants are generally limited to specific communities. A local board of directors usually determines which proposals are funded, although the donors may have some ability to direct certain funds.
- *Operating foundations* fund specific research programs or services which are determined by an independent board. These foundations may preselect recipient organizations and devise the projects they wish to have undertaken.

Know where to look for the foundation data which will indicate whether or not it is a good match for your proposal.

Unfortunately, there is no single source which lists all foundation grant programs. See Chapter 2 for a selection of resources which can lead you to appropriate foundations. Once you have established a select group for possible funding, contact those foundations to get information on projects, deadlines and application procedures.

Confer With Grantees

One step you can take in your foundation funding process is to contact those nonprofits similar to your own which have recently received grants from the foundations you are reviewing. Have a prepared checklist of questions such as these which can help you get an insider's view of what to expect in your search for funds.

- ❑ How did you go about applying for a grant?
- ❑ Did you contact the foundation office before submitting a letter of inquiry?
- ❑ Do you recommend a foundation visit prior to submitting a proposal?
- ❑ Is there a particular foundation officer you would recommend as an initial contact?
- ❑ Why did you pursue this foundation for a grant?
- ❑ What do you think tipped the scale in your favor?
- ❑ Did you have any linkage with this foundation through board members or volunteers?
- ❑ Did letters of support play any role in receiving your grant? Who provided letters?
- ❑ How long did it take between acceptance of your proposal and actual receipt of money?
- ❑ Would you recommend applying for a repeat grant from the same foundation?
- ❑ Did the foundation fund your entire request?
- ❑ What kind of follow-up and reporting is required or expected after funding?
- ❑ How long did the entire grant process take, from initial contact to the final report?

Grid System Prioritizes Funding Sources

The process of elimination and eventual prioritization of funding sources provides much greater focus in identifying and pursuing foundation and corporation grants. The use of a prospect prioritization grid can be a useful tool in this process.

- To begin, it's important to know your organization's needs and to develop a sense of funding priorities. Is library renovation, for instance, more important than new science labs? The ability to categorize needs will help to prioritize those projects to pursue most rigorously. You may want to form a grants committee to collectively prioritize funding needs. Those projects receiving an A rating, for instance, would be of highest priority, while those that receive a C rating would be desirable, but least important.

- Once your funding needs have been identified, initiate an ongoing commitment to review resources that publicize grants made by foundations and corporations.

- List the foundations/corporations whose grants are in line with the funding projects you wish to pursue.

- If available, include the names of one or two organizations that received funding, in case you choose to contact them for further information.

- Finally, check those categories matching the foundation or corporate grant with the appropriate organizational needs.

A grid-format report like this will help focus your funding efforts on those foundations and corporations that relate to your needs and programs.

Content not available in this edition

Know How to Use and Understand 990s

The IRS requires all private foundations to file tax returns (990-PF forms) annually, and to make these forms available to the public. The returns contain basic information about the foundations, including listings of grants and trustees. This information can be useful for fundraisers who work with foundations, and the forms often include more detail than can be found in directories.

GuideStar is the main source for researching 990s online. Searches are free, although additional information is also available for subscribers.

Although the details will vary from one foundation to the next, there are several key areas of information on 990s:

- The contact information **(1)** on the first page of the document contains the basics, including name, address and type of organization.

- The fair market value of the assets **(2)**, which is next to the contact information, is a guide to the size of the foundation.

- The main points to note in the financial summary **(3)** are the total revenues, total expenses and disbursements, and net income.

- The section which includes personnel information **(4)** generally includes a list of officers and directors, along with any compensation. This is especially helpful if you have a connection with one of the key foundation people.

- The listing of grants **(5)** will give you an idea of foundation priorities and giving ranges. These listings do not always give details of the specific programs which were funded, but the types of recipients can be a guide.

If you stick to the key areas mentioned here, the information

found in a 990-PF, along with a copy of the guidelines and an annual report, may be all the background you need to approach a foundation for funding.

The IRS requires all private foundations to file tax returns (990-PF forms) annually, and to make these forms available to the public.

continued on page 62

Content not available in this edition

continued from page 61

Content not available in this edition

Content not available in this edition

Advisory Boards Welcome Involvement, Lead to Major Gifts

Identify and mine specific ways to connect individuals, businesses and industries to your organization to engage them in your cause.

Purdue University (West Lafayette, IN) hosts 34 industrial advisory boards that share research with corporate partners and help build relationships that lead to funding.

Each advisory board is tied to a different field of research, such as food sciences, computer science, engineering education, and computer information and technology, says Betsy Liley, assistant vice president for corporate and foundation relations.

Liley says many of the boards are structured around membership levels, which range from $2,500 to $80,000 per year. Average group size is 15 to 20. The annual gifts help pay for the cost of running each board, including a salary for a paid staff member.

In addition to the annual membership gift, many companies sponsor research projects and fund scholarships for students in fields of interest to their advisory board, Liley says. While individual board structures vary, generally, each board sponsors research as a group, attends two meetings a year and may participate in annual job recruitment fairs.

"If the company's interest is in students and recruiting, they will be interested in supporting scholarships that will get them in front of students," she says. "If their interest is in research, they will want to sponsor research projects that expose them to our experts and allow them direct access to our research."

Advisory board members are at the corporate management level. Specific departments or colleges — many of which already have relationships with those departments or colleges through previous research funding — identify prospective corporate partners or attendance at job recruitment fairs on campus.

"Corporate involvement helps shape our curriculum, keeps us up to date on the skills our students need to have to compete in the job market, and guides our research," says Liley. "Our corporate partners have access to our research and our top students, and get to interact with their peers and partner with them on projects."

Source: Betsy Liley, Assistant Vice President for Corporate & Foundation Relations, Purdue University, West Lafayette, IN. E-mail: bliley@purdue.edu

Industrial advisory boards at Purdue University (West Lafayette, IN), allow the university to share research with corporate partners.

Content not available in this edition

Content not available in this edition

Prospect Research Fundamentals — 4th Edition

Whether preparing for a capital campaign, selecting prospect groups for a wealth screening, or simply evaluating your organization's overall fundraising potential, prioritizing prospects is a key aspect of making the most of your staff time and efforts. That prioritization process involves much more than wealth assessment.

Regularly Review Your Top 100 Individual Prospects

Your top 100 prospects represent a dynamic, ever-changing group of individuals.

To properly rank and steward this important group, review your list regularly — at least monthly — and prioritize who should remain, who should be added and who should be moved to a lesser priority (or inactive) level.

Include in this review process criteria related to both capability and inclination to give.

Give staff and highly involved board members a list of your current top prospects, along with additional names not presently on that list. Instruct those persons to first review the list individually, assigning a rating of 1, 2 or 3 beside each prospect's name — 1 meaning keep on the list, 2 meaning discuss for possible change in status, and 3 meaning recommendation to add to the list.

Then, meet as a group and compare your thoughts, and adjust your top 100 prospect list accordingly.

Evaluate Ways to Prioritize Prospects

There are a number of aspects to grouping your donor and prospect base, and several techniques for which you will get similar results. The following summary can be used to guide you through the major parts of this process and help you find the cream of the crop.

Goal Setting

As with any major project, the first step is to define your goals:

- Are you preparing for a major or annual campaign, embarking on a direct mail solicitation program, or setting up a group to be contacted for a phonathon? The end product will determine what type of group you are hoping to find, and therefore will help define your search criteria.
- How large a group of donors do you need to fulfill your fundraising goal? Keep in mind the number of staff and volunteers you have to manage those prospects.
- What size gifts do you expect to get from the donors in this group? Anticipating both the number and range of gift sizes will help define the approach you take in prospect prioritization.

Internal Reports

One of the easiest and most effective methods for prioritizing your prospects is through the use of computer reports which are designed in-house.

- Segment your donor base by past giving levels, consistency, types and programs.
- Group together those with similar professions, age ranges, geographic locations or interests.
- Designate groups with board memberships.
- Indicate volunteer relationships.
- Set aside your organization's faculty and/or staff for a separate campaign component.

Database Screening

If you feel the data you have in-house is insufficient for your needs, there are vendors who can provide additional information on your prospects and donors. Costs and data analysis services vary with each vendor, and are generally based on the number of records you want them to process. Most of them will run a test for you on a select sample from your database to give you an idea of the results you could get. The main vendors include **Blackbaud Analytics**, **DonorCast**, **Grenzebach Glier & Associates** and **WealthEngine**. Their products range from demographics and wealth rankings to specific stockholding and real estate data.

Peer Screening Sessions

Using the results from internal reports or database screening services, you can further refine your list of prospects by conducting peer screening sessions. These are meetings that you set up with various groups to rate the potential giving of prospects they know.

Involve Researchers From the Start

The key to success in any of these processes is to involve your research staff in the project from the very beginning.

- Get input from all development staff at the planning stage.
- Make sure your researchers participate in the process and attend all rating sessions. They can document any additional details which might be discussed, and help interpret reports for the volunteers.
- Allow enough time and staff to follow up on the results of these projects. The ability to use the data once it is collected is as important as having the data.
- Determine up front who will be responsible for analyzing the data once it is collected. Some of the database screening vendors offer varying levels of analysis support as part of their services.
- Decide how your staff will use the data. Divide the prioritized prospect pool among your staff members as soon as possible, and set goals and deadlines.

Develop a System for Prioritizing Your Top Prospects

There are many methods used to prioritize prospects, some more objective than others. Whatever method you use, it's important to prioritize would-be donors based on both capability and inclination to support your cause.

Here's an example of a prospect rating form. This form serves to measure both an individual's ability and likelihood to make a major gift.

Criteria used to rate prospects on this form include:

1. **Common interests.** Does the prospect exhibit interest in the kinds of objectives your organization attempts to address?

2. **Financial ability.** Can the prospect afford to make a major gift by your standards?

3. **Commitment to philanthropy.** Any history of the prospect giving to other causes?

4. **Commitment to your organization.** Has the prospect exhibited any past commitment to your organization (e.g., past contributor or involvement in programs)?

5. **Linkages with your organization.** Has the prospect held an office with your nonprofit or been served as a client of your organization? Does he/she have friends or family who have linkages to you?

6. **Time window.** Is the time right for the prospect to make a major gift? Examples affecting time window might include: inheritance, sale of certain assets, divorce.

7. **Personality.** How can the individual's personality affect his/her interest in making a gift? Is the individual driven by a strong ego? Is he/she caring? Personality traits will influence the likelihood of giving.

8. **Past solicitation success.** Has the prospect contributed to your cause in the past? Is there a long or brief history of giving? Has she/he made a previous major gift?

9. **Common politics/philosophy.** Do the political/philosophical beliefs of this individual coincide with the mission and goals of your organization? Does the prospect stand far to the left or right politically? Where is your nonprofit positioned politically?

Weights are assigned to each rating criteria and then added. In this case, the highest possible score one can receive is 85.

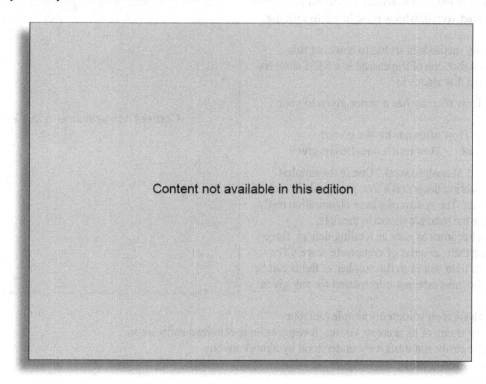

Content not available in this edition

Rating Systems Overview

A rating system is a way of applying a number or code to prospects to categorize them according to their appropriate places in a gift table or major gifts program.

Setting up a rating system for your prospects and donors can help you prioritize them for solicitations, and you can separate them by timing or gift size.

The process for determining ratings can be simple or complex, but needs to be tailored to your organization's needs and your constituency. Ratings can come from many sources, including an analysis of your database, an internal committee review, peer screening sessions, vendor database screenings or surveys.

Although ratings tend to be subjective to a certain extent, you can apply some science to your methodology. Ratings can be based on total giving capability, past giving to your organization, interest and involvement. Your organization may want to determine what aspects should hold more weight when scoring individual prospects. These could include wealth indicators such as stock holdings and private company ownership or volunteer affiliations.

Try to find a way to tie your ratings into your main prospect database. Once a rating system is established, it needs to be regularly updated and kept consistent.

When asking a group of individuals to rate a predetermined list of prospects according to their financial capability, allow participants the option of anonymity. Results may be more honest if participants are not required to give their names.

Rank Major Gift Prospects With an RFM Analysis

You've just finished assembling your list of top major gift prospects. Now what?

Whether your list has a dozen names or a hundred, the next step is to rank them in terms of potential impact on your organization. In other words, who is most likely to give the largest gift?

There are many methods of trying to tease out this critical information, but one of the easiest is a RFM analysis. RFM is an acronym that stands for:

- **Recency** — How recently has a donor given to your organization?
- **Frequency** — How often has he/she given?
- **Monetary value** — How much does he/she give?

How does an RFM analysis work? One of the simplest schemes involves scoring donors on a four-point scale in each of those three categories. The system of a large organization might look something like the example shown to the right.

Grading then becomes as easy as totaling donors' three scores and ranking them in order of composite score. (The parameters of each field and even the number of fields can be adjusted to give the most relevant information for any given organization.)

An RFM analysis is an admittedly simple tool, but that very simplicity is one of its greatest virtues. It requires no specialized software to produce and can be easily and intuitively understood by almost anyone.

If your organization is struggling to figure out what prospects to target, why not give an RFM analysis a try?

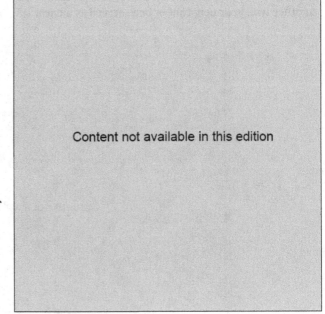

Content not available in this edition

Identify, Prioritize Funders

Maureen Martin, senior director of foundation relations for the University of Michigan (Ann Arbor, MI), answers some questions about how they identify and prioritize foundation funders:

What steps do you go through to identify and then prioritize your most likely foundation supporters?

"As in any kind of fundraising, our best prospects for future support are our current and recent donors. So we begin there first, watching for whether any foundations have decreased or halted their giving across time, whether there's been a change in pattern of giving or in staffing. Then we watch closely any and all foundations that are active in our region — either within the state or the larger multi-state region. Finally, we peruse the databases of foundation grants and foundation news items for tips on major funding initiatives from elsewhere in the country. We prioritize by a combination of likelihood of success and size of potential gift/grant."

How do you identify funders in the first place, and then once you do, how do you go about prioritizing them based on importance/likelihood of a gift?

"We do as tight a read as possible of past grants, grant guidelines and programs, etc. So we undertake a deep review of the grants path of the foundation (for example, we can see whether the foundation gives grants nationally or has a few areas of focus, gives a lot or a few grants at scale, has ever funded in our home state, funds in areas in which we are particularly strong, etc.), and then work with faculty to understand if our work correlates to the foundation areas of interest/support. Our regional and donor prospects will always have the deepest review; then the larger but more geographically remote prospects will receive less frequent but also deep review perhaps three or four times a year."

Source: Maureen Martin, Senior Director, Foundation Relations, University of Michigan, Ann Arbor, MI. E-mail: martinms@umich.edu

Put Firm Numbers on Major Gift Solicitation

Outstanding fundraising comes not from guesswork but from hard data that goes back to the earliest stages of the solicitation process, says Christina Pulawski, principal of Christina Pulawski Consulting (Chicago, IL).

Pulawski says systematic and reliable fundraising includes understanding and calculating your organization's prospect yield — the percentage of solicited prospects who donate at the level you suggest.

Imagine you have 20 promising prospects identified, she says. Of these, you might be successful in approaching only 16 of them. Of these 16, you may qualify only 12 as having sufficient capacity and interest in your cause. Of the 12, you may succeed in actively cultivating only eight. Of the eight, cultivation might proceed far enough to solicit only four of them. And of those four, only one might say yes to the amount you request. Your average yield, then, is one out of 20, or 5 percent.

Yield is a valuable metric in itself, but it can also be used to enhance major gift forecasting. Multiplying the total number of proposals planned over a certain period by the

fundraising process (the yield of prospects qualified from the total, etc.) will aid in understanding where your processes may be able to be improved, or where more or better information may be needed, says Pulawski.

Yield is a valuable metric in itself, but it can also be used to enhance major gift forecasting. Multiplying the total number of proposals planned over a certain period of time by rate prospects are actually solicited by your organization, the solicitation yield and the average dollar amount of major gifts gives a reliable estimate of the revenue you can realistically expect to generate:

$$\text{(planned proposals)} \times \text{(solicitation rate)} \times \text{(yield)} \times \text{(average gift)} = \text{(total projected commitments)}$$

Pulawski says it's important to remember that at least six months to a year's worth of accurate data are often needed to generate remotely reliable projections.

Source: Christina Pulawski, Principal, Christina Pulawski Consulting, Chicago, IL. E-mail: c-pulawski@comcast.net

'Inclination to Give' Part of Prospect Research Equation

Important as it is to identify and measure a prospect's financial capability, it's also important to gauge a prospect's inclination to give. Whether you're meeting with a focus group or steering committee or confining your research to staff, categorizing perceptions about an individual's inclination to give helps prioritize prospects and determine cultivation steps and timing for eventual solicitation.

Examples of inclination levels you can use as a gauging tool include:

❑ **High inclination** — More than likely has already given generously in the past. The individual has an obvious linkage to your organization (e.g., board member, donor, regular patron). He/she may be highly involved with your organization in some capacity.

❑ **Above-average inclination** — The individual has some degree of linkage to the organization and may or may not have contributed in the past.

❑ **Average inclination** — Although the individual may appear favorably disposed to the organization, there is no history to indicate he/she has any ties or interest. He/she may have been supportive of other philanthropic causes.

❑ **Below-average inclination** — Some past action (e.g., a past development call, something that was said by the prospect) indicates that the prospect may look unfavorably toward the organization even though he/she has supported other causes.

❑ **Little or no inclination** — The individual has no interest in the organization and little or no history of past support to other charitable causes.